# Dear Family Member,

Many children think that math = difficulty. Scholastic's *100 Math Activities Kids Need to Do by 1st Grade* will help your first grader realize that understanding + practice = math success.

Children need practice in order to develop mathematical thinking and mathematical skills. They need engaging examples in order to make abstract math ideas concrete. They need rich, varied opportunities in order to work successfully with math concepts and symbols. Your first grader will find all of that in our colorful, educational, *fun* activities.

The 100 activities in this workbook will help your child build his or her understanding of and facility with the key concepts and operations involved in

- number sense
- addition and subtraction
- measurement
- geometry
- time
- money
- organizing data

A Math Skills list, on page 224, highlights the math skills in the activities in this workbook. These essential skills relate to the math curricula and standardized tests your child will be exposed to in school.

We've included a sheet of reusable math stickers, which your child can use to create number or word equations, solve number problems, and engage in all kinds of creative math play.

You are an important part of your child's math education, so we've also provided a few suggestions below for easily integrating math into your daily routine.

Scholastic's *100 Math Activities Kids Need to Do by 1st Grade* will give your child math competence . . . and confidence. Enjoy!

Jean Feiwel
Scholastic Publisher, Senior Vice President

## Parent Tips

- Read the directions on each activity page with your first grader. Make sure your child knows what to do. When he or she solves a problem, ask, "How do you know?" The more reasoning your child gives, the better.
- Put the math stickers where your child can easily see and reach them. Challenge your child to solve a new sticker equation each day.
- Play math games while you're driving, preparing meals, waiting in line, sitting in waiting rooms. They might include
  - saying a number and asking which number(s) comes before or after it
  - saying several numbers and asking your child to say them in order, highest to lowest and lowest to highest
  - starting to skip count by 2s, 5s, and 10s and asking your child to continue
  - posing simple addition or subtraction problems
  - playing "I spy" based on geometric shapes
- Play sorting games while doing the laundry.
- While grocery shopping, ask your child to compare products by size or price. Ask which ones cost more than $1, which cost less.
- Have a set of plastic measuring cups in the bathtub or swimming pool for your child to play with.
- Make a paper-plate clock with your child. Play "what time is it when we . . ."; name an activity and ask your child to show the time; or write down a time and ask your child to show it on the clock. Take turns doing this.

**Editor:** Sheila Keenan
**Art Director:** Nancy Sabato
**Managing Editor:** Karyn Browne
**Production Editor:** Bonnie Cutler
**Project Management:** Kevin Callahan, BNGO Books
**Composition:** Kevin Callahan, Patty Harris, Tony Lee, Daryl Richardson

**Copyeditor/Proofreader:** Geraldine Albert, Abigail Winograd
**Cover:** Red Herring Design
**Editorial Consultant:** Dale A. Beltzner, Jr., Elementary Math Specialist, Lower Milford Elementary School, Coopersburg, Pennsylvania
**Activity Pages Writer:** Carolyn Ford Brunetto
**Activity Pages Illustrator:** Jackie Snider

0-439-56679-7

12 11 10 9 8 7 6 5 4 3 2                4 5 6 7 8 9/0

Printed in the U.S.A.                **40**
First printing, May 2004

**PHOTO CREDITS**
**ALAMY** 56 (bottom): Peter Bowater; 58–59 (jelly beans): foodfolio; 96: Focus Group, LLC; 97: Focus Group, LLC; 178 (girl reading): Rubberball Productions; 179 (child eating cereal): Peter Mumford; 212–213 (red car): Anthony Oliver/Image State, (gummy bear): Hans-Peter Moehlig; 217 (top): Steven Hamblin, (bottom): Robert Harding World Imagery
**CORBIS** 34 (football): Corbis Royalty-Free; 155 (CD): Corbis Royalty-Free; 202 (football): Corbis Royalty-Free
**GETTY** 22: Rubberball Productions; 48 (top): Photodisc, (middle): Rubberball Productions; 84–85 (darker monkey): Photodisc; 90–91 (buttons): Photodisc; 102 (blue butterfly): Photodisc; 103 (both): Photodisc; 111 (bottom): Photodisc; 131 (two girls in pajamas): Rubberball Productions; 133 (flowers): Photodisc; 142–143 (rubber duck, blue gift box): Photodisc; 143 (blue gift box): Photodisc; 154 (checker board, tepee): Photodisc; 155 (cracker): Photodisc; 172–173 (darker monkey): Photodisc; 172 (two girls tying their shoes): Ryan McVay, (two girls in pajamas): Rubberball Productions; 179 (baseball game): Photodisc; 183 (lower right): Photodisc; 198 (buttons): Photodisc; 198 (blue butterfly): Photodisc; 202 (basketball): Ryan McVay/Photodisc; 212–213 (buttons): Photodisc
**PHOTO EDIT** 56 (top): Myrleen Ferguson Cate; 106 (all) David Young Wolff; 112 (top): David Young Wolff; 133 (two girls sharing snack): Amy Etra; 143 (star): Amy Etra; 179 (sunset): Myrleen Ferguson Cate, (children exiting school bus): Tom McCarthy; 183 (top left): Myrleen Ferguson Cate, (top right): Jeff Greenberg, (lower left): Michael Newman
**PICTUREQUEST** 36 (sandwich): C Squared Studios/Photodisc; 44–45: C Squared Studios/Photodisc; 84–85 (lighter monkey): Ryan McVay/Photodisc; 112 (streamers): C Squared Studios/Photodisc; 118: C Squared Studios/Photodisc; 131 (roller blades): C Squared Studios/Photodisc; 142–143 (musical triangle): C Squared Studios/Photodisc; 172–173 (lighter monkey): Ryan McVay/Photodisc; 198 (roller blades): C Squared Studios/Photodisc

**MASTERFILE** 110 (bottom): Graham French
**PHOTO RESEARCHERS** 132 (girl with dog): Catherine Ursillo
**SODA** 11: John Lei via SODA; 34 (soccer ball): Photodisc via SODA; 36 (pink plate, green plate): David Franck via SODA; 49 (from top to bottom): Image 100 via SODA, Photodisc via SODA, Dick Clintsman via SODA, Image 100 via SODA; 62–63 (cookies): Ana Esperanza via SODA; 66–67 (teddy bears): David Waitz via SODA; 70–71 (oranges, apples, bananas): Photodisc via SODA, (watermelon): Peter Neumann via SODA; 74–75 (sea shells): John Lei via SODA; 92 (top): Photodisc via SODA, (bottom): Digital Vision via SODA; 93 (both): Photodisc via SODA; 102 (black butterfly): Photodisc via SODA; 110 (top four images from top to bottom): Photodisc via SODA, Image 100 via SODA, Image 100 via SODA, Photodisc via SODA; 111 (middle left): Image 100 via SODA, (middle right): Dick Clintsman via SODA; 130 (piano): Artville via SODA; (cake): Photodisc via SODA; 131 (cupcake): Photodisc via SODA; 132 (thermometer): David Lawrence via SODA, (boy with bucket): Photodisc via SODA; 133 (girl with red striped shirt): Digital Vision via SODA; 142–143 (soccer ball): Photodisc via SODA; 54 (beach ball): Digital Vision via SODA, (fabric): Ken Karp via SODA, (watermelon): Peter Neumann via SODA, (die): Stephen J. Carr via SODA; 198 (bear cookie): Ana Esperanza via SODA, (beach ball): Digital Vision via SODA, (cupcake): Photodisc via SODA, (banana): John Bessler via SODA; 199 (stamp): USPS via SODA, (tennis ball): John Lei via SODA, (orange, beach bucket, hammer): Photodisc via SODA, (watermelon): Peter Neumann via SODA; 202 (baseball, soccer ball, cake): Photodisc via SODA, (tennis ball): John Lei via SODA; 208–209: Photodisc via SODA; 212–213 (seashells): John Lei via SODA
**SUPERSTOCK** pages; 48 (bottom): Vincent Hobbs; 111 (top left): Tom Rosenthal (top right): Vincent Hobbs; 132 (children sledding): Jerry Amster; 133 (boy with snowman): Jianj Jin

# Contents

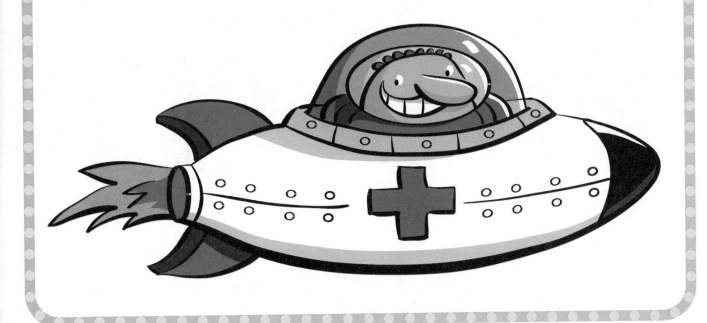

# Beep, Beep!

How many clowns came out of the car? Write the number.

_____

_____

_____

_____

_____

How many clowns are
left in the car? _____

# Up a Tree

How many birds are in each tree?
Write the number.

2

1

0

6

8

4

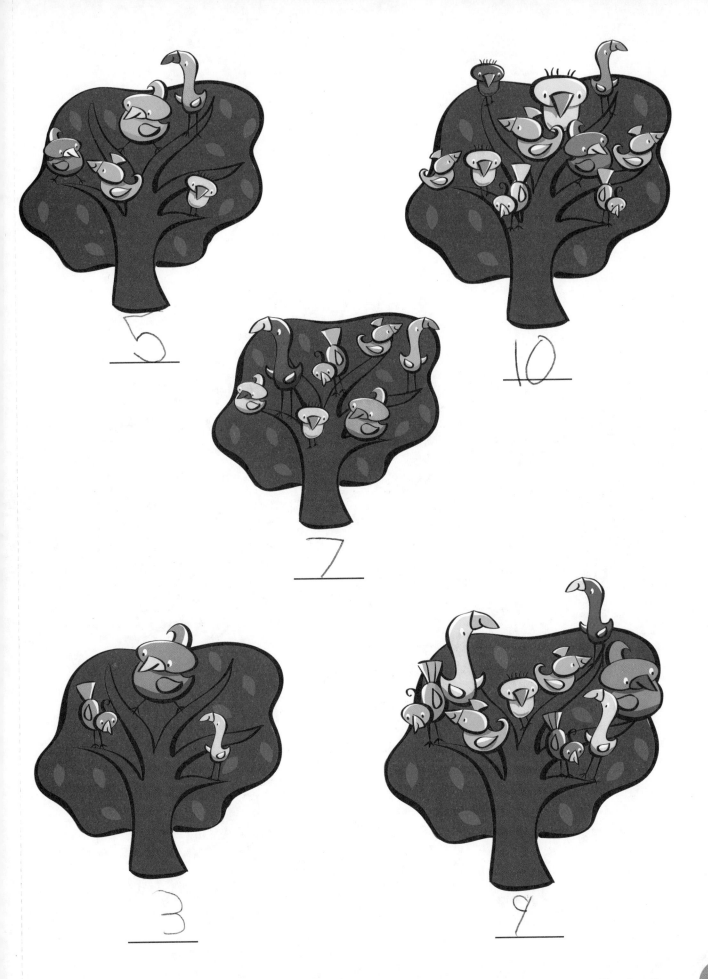

# Count the Carrots

How many carrots are in each bunch?
Draw a line to the number.

11

12

13

14

15

16

17

18

19

20

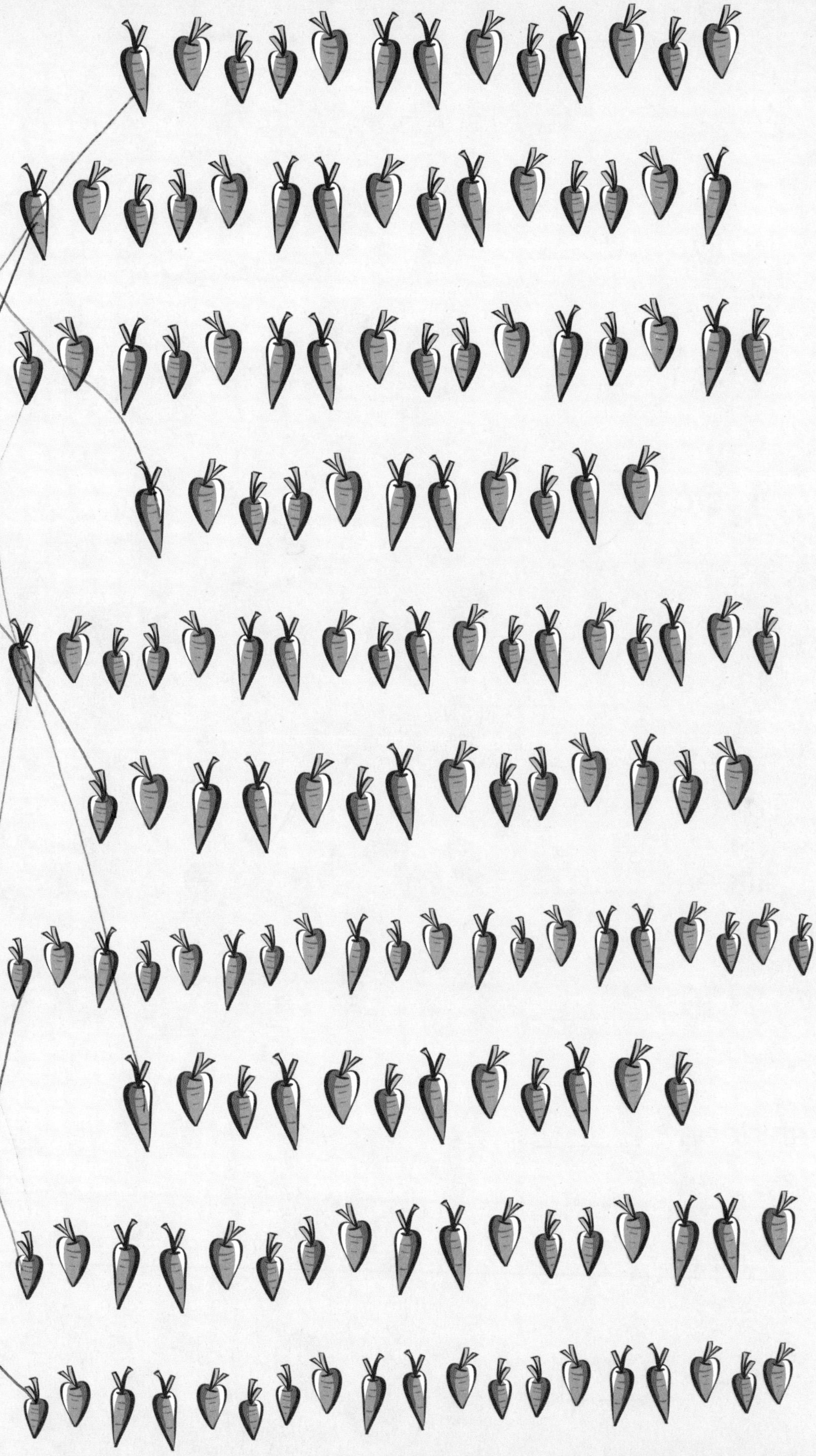

# By the Sea

Write the number for each word.

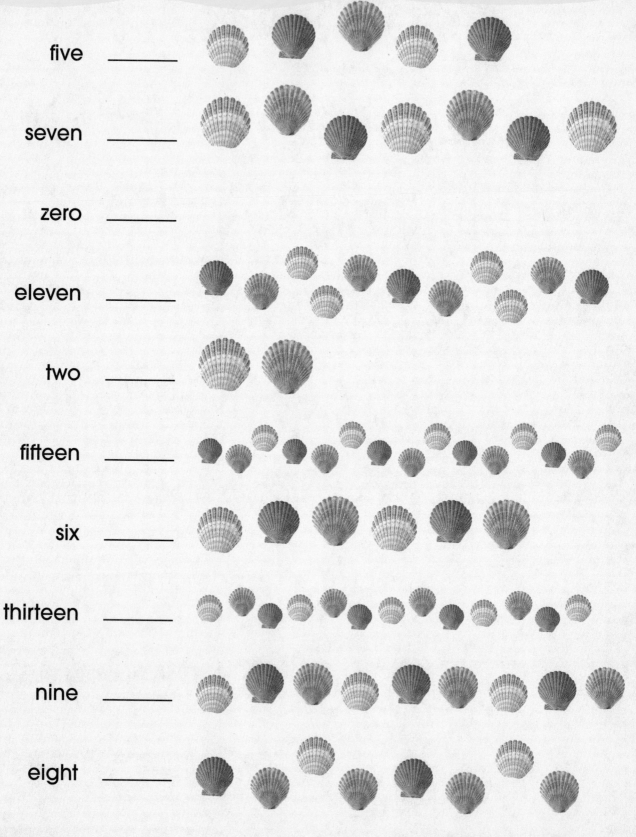

five _____

seven _____

zero _____

eleven _____

two _____

fifteen _____

six _____

thirteen _____

nine _____

eight _____

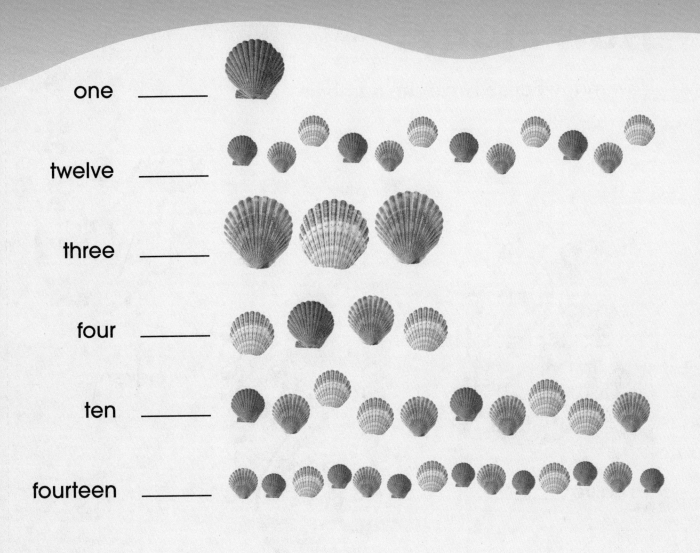

one _____

twelve _____

three _____

four _____

ten _____

fourteen _____

Which of the numbers above come **after** 10?
Write them in order.

_____

_____

_____

_____

_____

# How Many?

How many balls? Write the number.

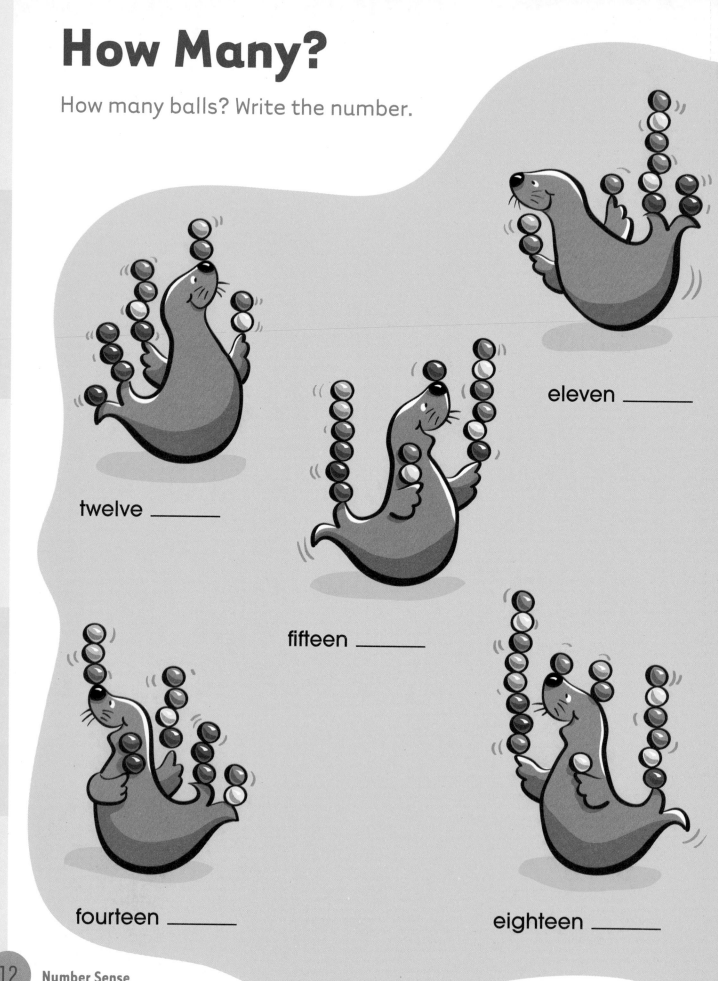

twelve _____

eleven _____

fifteen _____

fourteen _____

eighteen _____

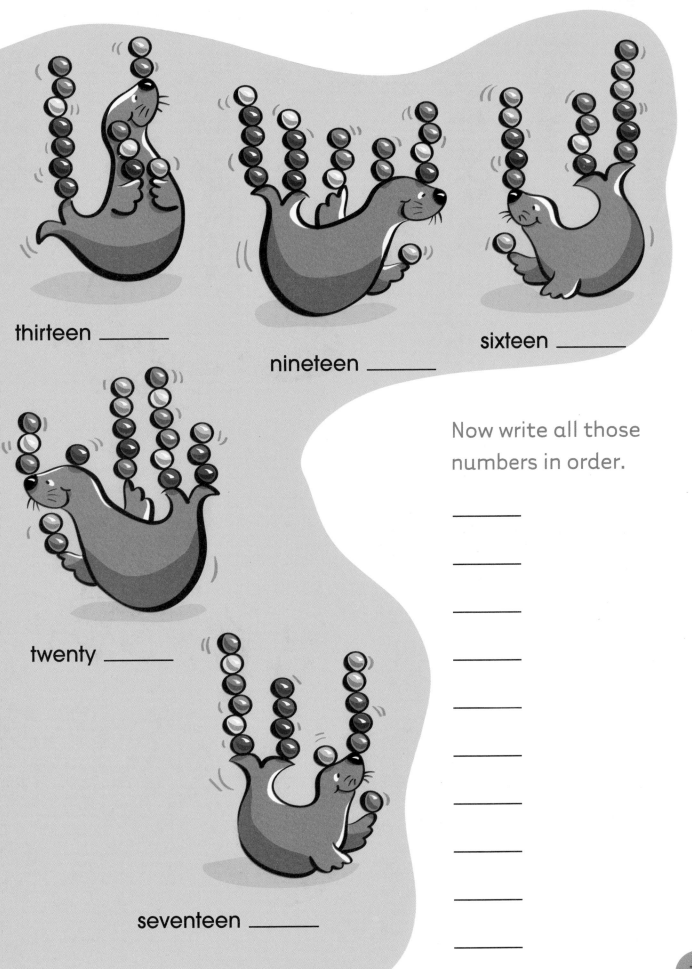

thirteen _____

nineteen _____

sixteen _____

twenty _____

seventeen _____

Now write all those numbers in order.

_____

_____

_____

_____

_____

_____

_____

_____

# Ant Parade

Each ant needs three numbers in order.
Write the missing numbers on the lines.

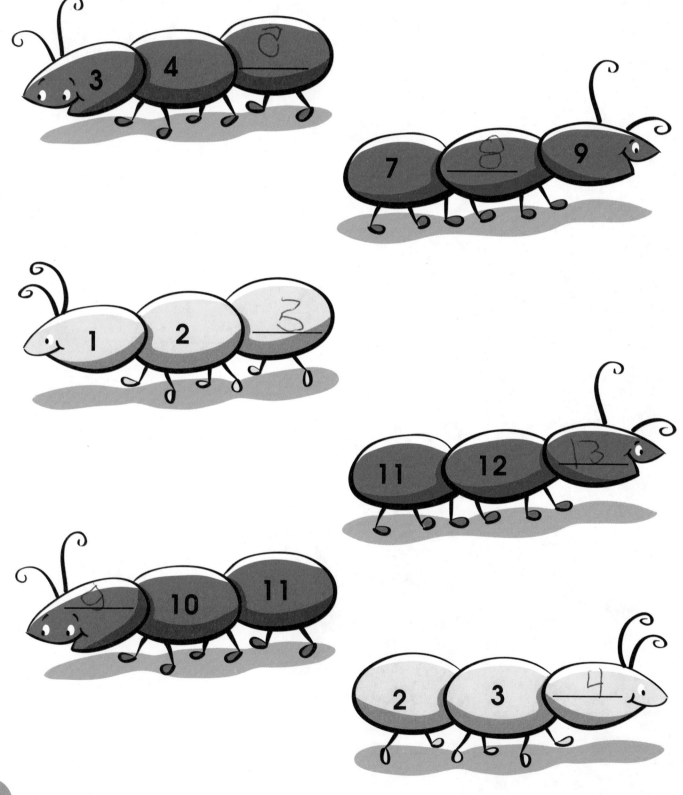

**Number Sense**

# Hop to It!

Draw lines to match the number
with the number word.

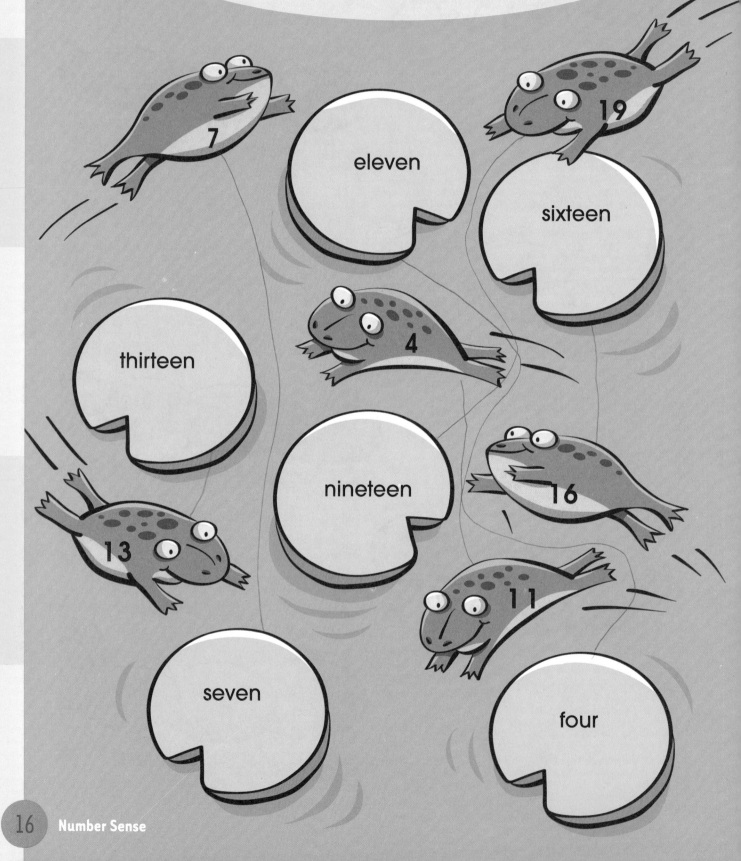

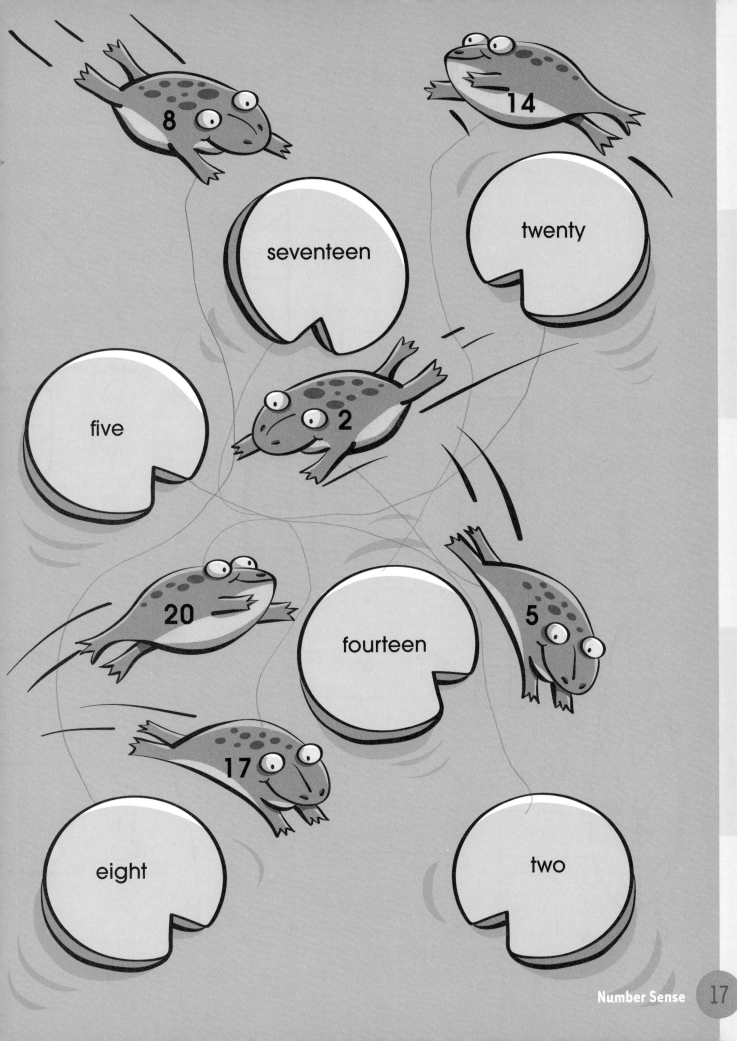

# Picture This

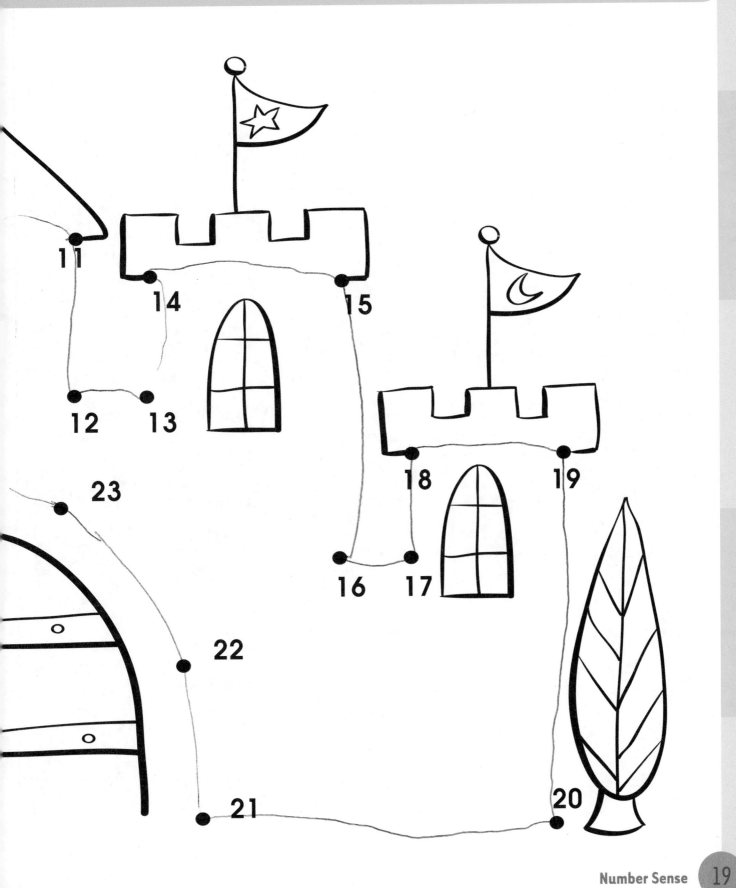

# Please Take Your Seats

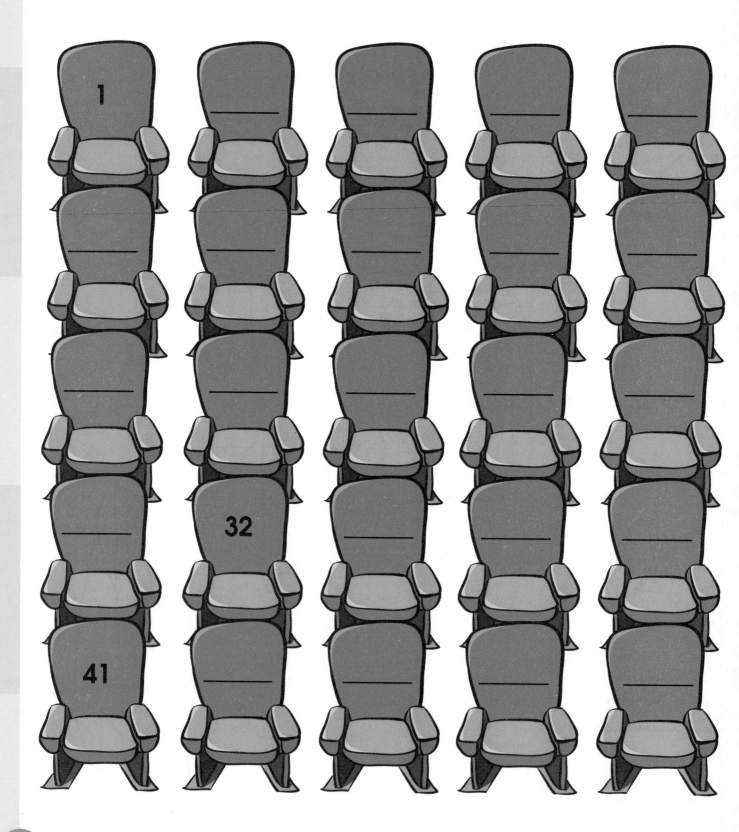

# Count from 1 to 50.
## Write the missing numbers on the lines.

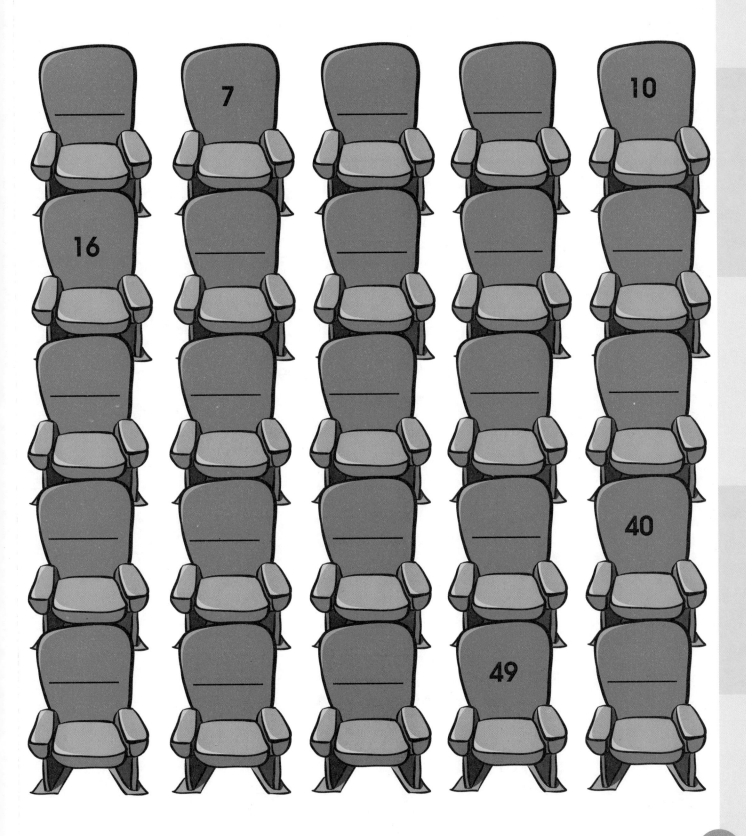

# Yes!

Read each number and word.
Do they mean the same thing? (Circle) **yes** or **no**.

| | | | |
|---|---|---|---|
| 3 | three | (yes) | no |
| 15 | sixteen | yes | (no) |
| 10 | ten | (yes) | no |
| 7 | seven | (yes) | no |
| 5 | fifteen | yes | (no) |
| 20 | twenty | (yes) | no |
| 12 | ten | yes | (no) |
| 1 | one | (yes) | no |

| 19 | nine | yes | (no) |
| 8 | eight | (yes) | no |
| 11 | one | yes | (no) |
| 13 | thirteen | (yes) | no |
| 6 | six | (yes) | no |
| 5 | five | (yes) | no |
| 18 | eight | yes | (no) |
| 16 | thirteen | yes | (no) |
| 7 | seven | (yes) | no |
| 14 | fourteen | (yes) | no |
| 0 | one | yes | (no) |
| 10 | ten | (yes) | no |
| 9 | nineteen | yes | (no) |
| 11 | eleven | (yes) | no |
| 2 | twenty | yes | (no) |
| 15 | five | yes | (no) |

# All Aboard!

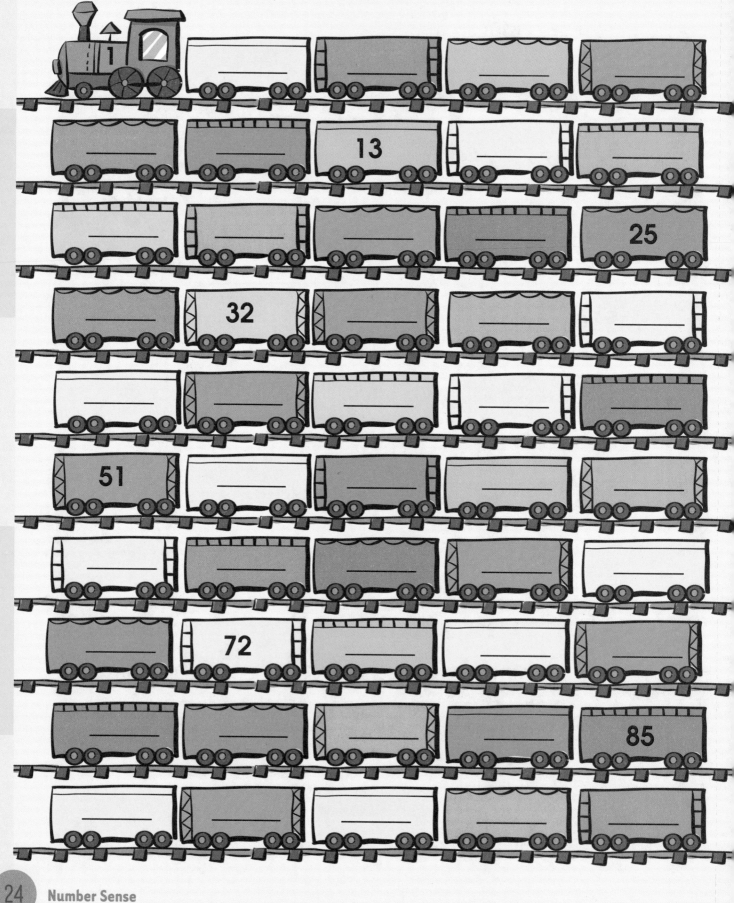

Count from 1 to 100. Write the missing numbers.

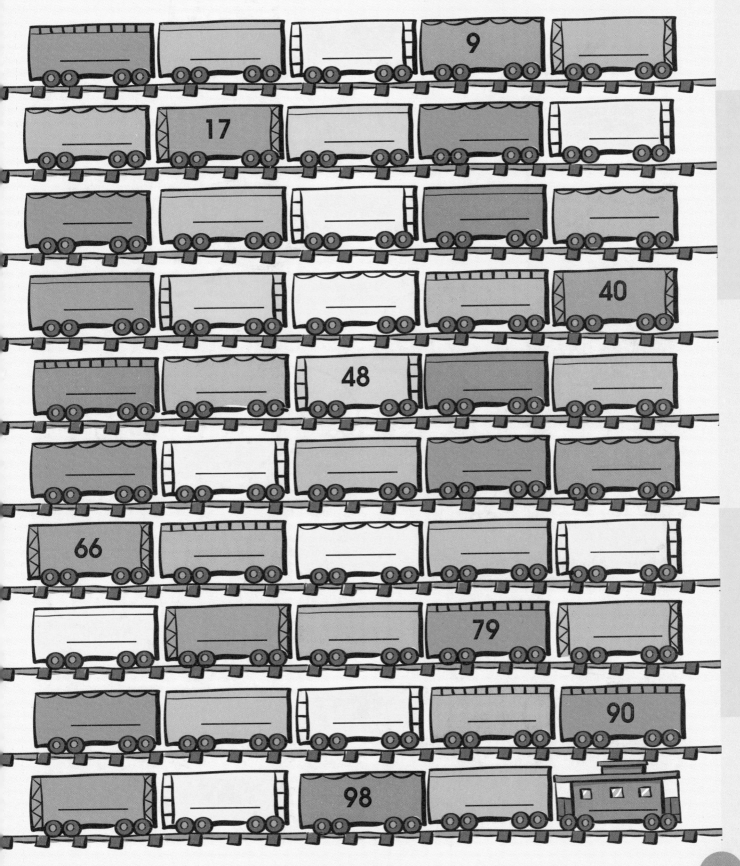

# What Comes Before?

Write the missing numbers.

1  2  3

13  14  15

8  9  10

24  25  26

48  49  50

30  31  32

87  88  89

52  53  54

68 69 70

9 10 11

75 76 77

20 21 22

17 18 19 20

97 98 99 100

49 50 51 52

88 89 90 91

# Quick Counting by 2s

You can count quickly if you count by **2s**.
Help these kittens count all their mittens.

_____

_____

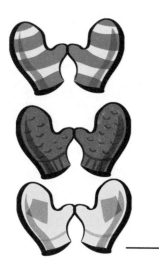

_____

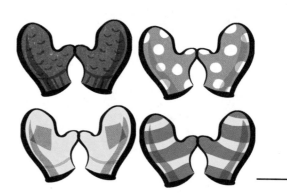

_____

_____

_____

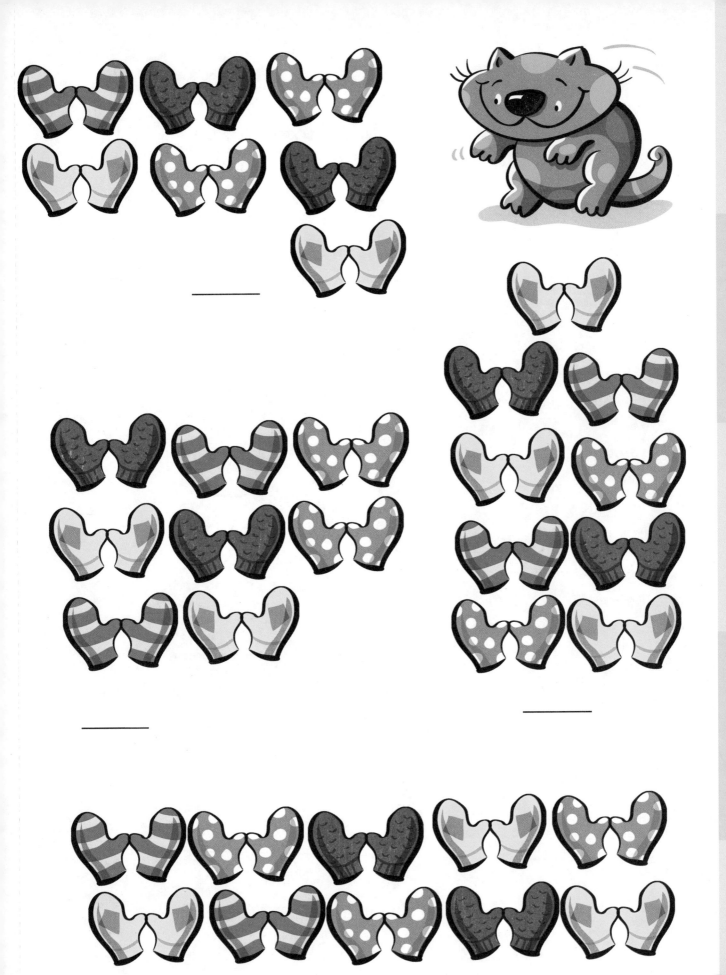

_____

_____

_____

_____

# Growing Numbers by 5s

Counting by **5s** is a quick way get to 50.
Write the missing numbers.

# Digging Numbers by 10s

Counting by **10s** is an easy way to deal with large numbers.
Write the missing numbers.

_10_

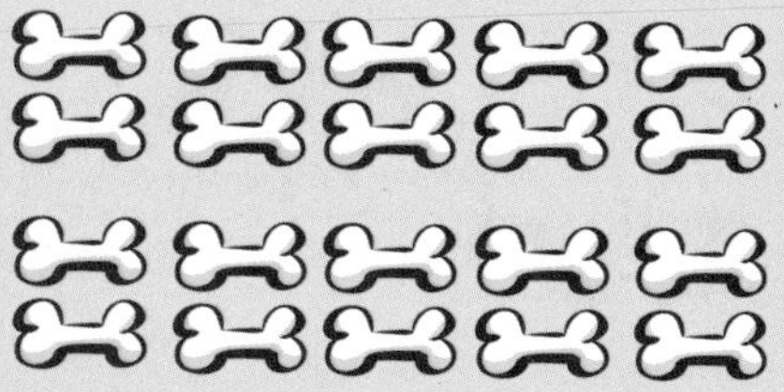

_20_

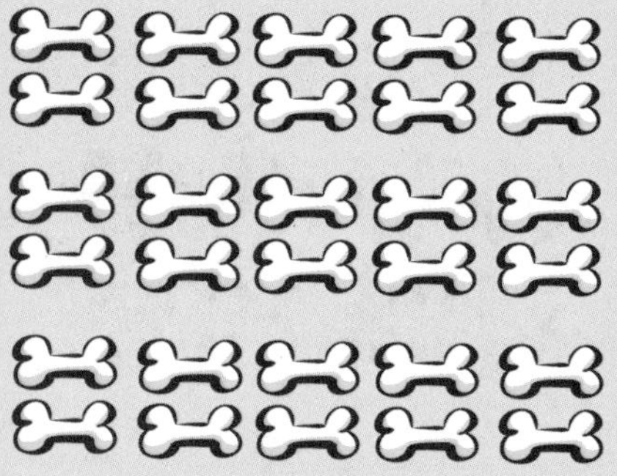

_30_

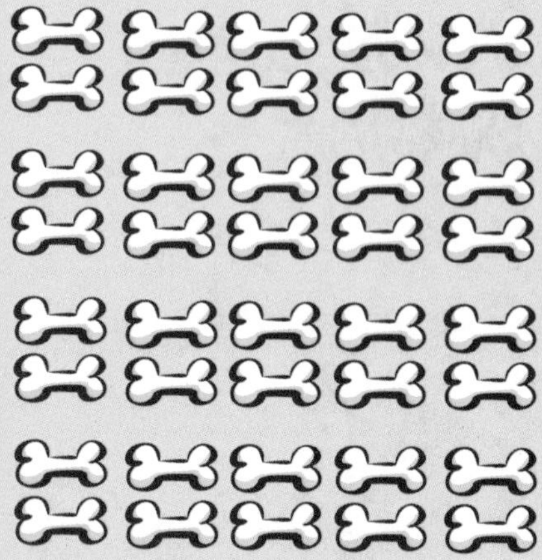

_40_

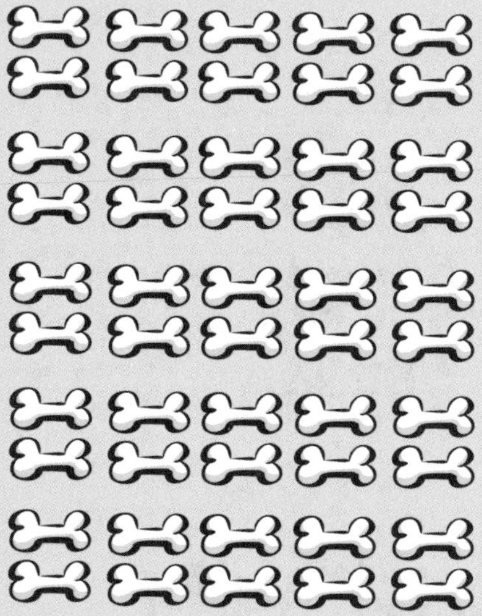

_50_

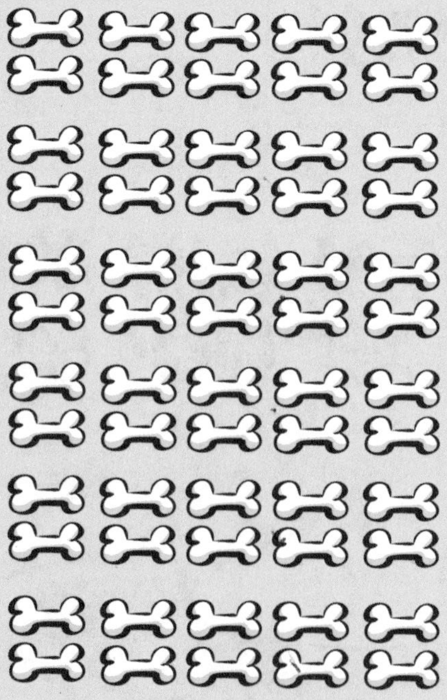

_60_

70

80

90

100

# What a Kick!

Count the **10s**. Count the **1s**. Add them together.
Write the answer in the box.

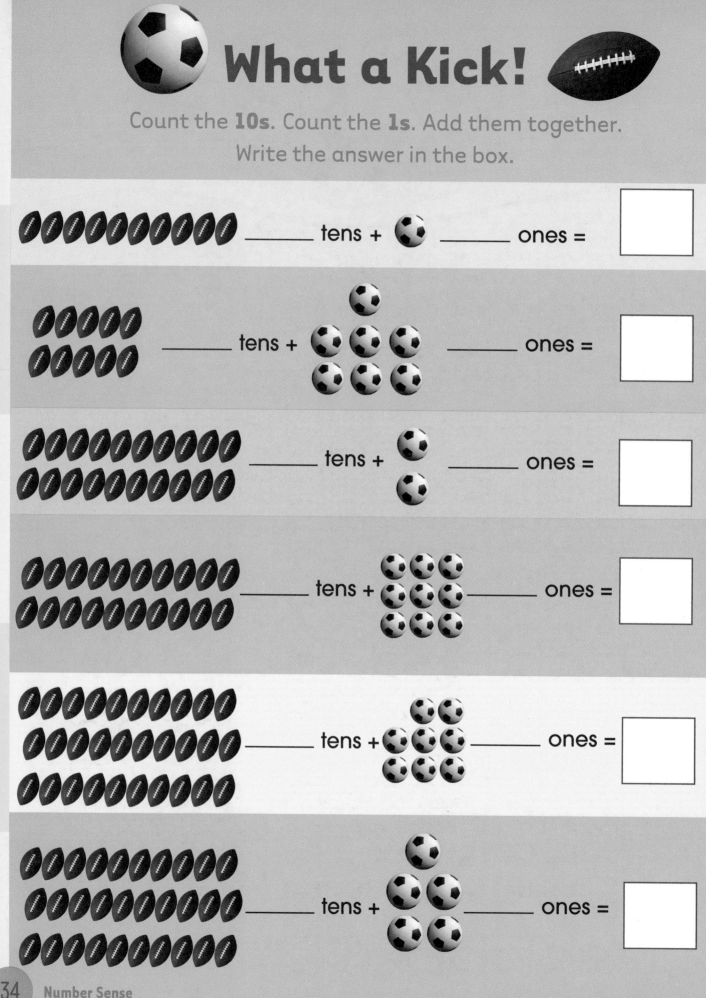

_____ tens + _____ ones = ☐

_____ tens + _____ ones = ☐

_____ tens + _____ ones = ☐

_____ tens + _____ ones = ☐

_____ tens + _____ ones = ☐

_____ tens + _____ ones = ☐

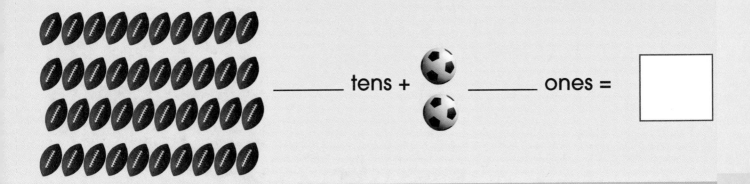 _____ tens + 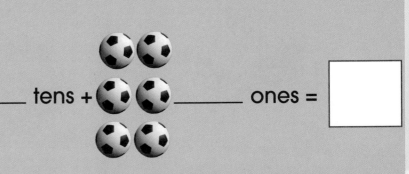 _____ ones = ☐

_____ tens +  _____ ones = ☐

_____ tens + 🖤 _____ ones = ☐

_____ tens + 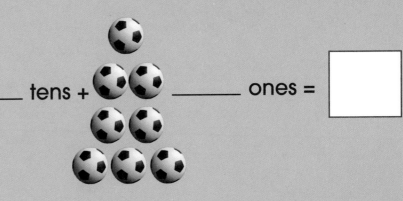 _____ ones = ☐

# Meal Mix-Up

Draw a line from each sandwich to the correct plate.

39

7 tens, 8 ones

2 tens, 7 ones

41

3 tens, 9 ones

78

4 tens, 1 one

27

94

5 tens, 5 ones

6 tens, 7 ones

67

9 tens, 4 ones

55

46

4 tens, 6 ones

# Fly, Fly Away

Circle the flower on each stem that has **more** butterflies.

# Let's Shop!

Circle the group that has **fewer** things.

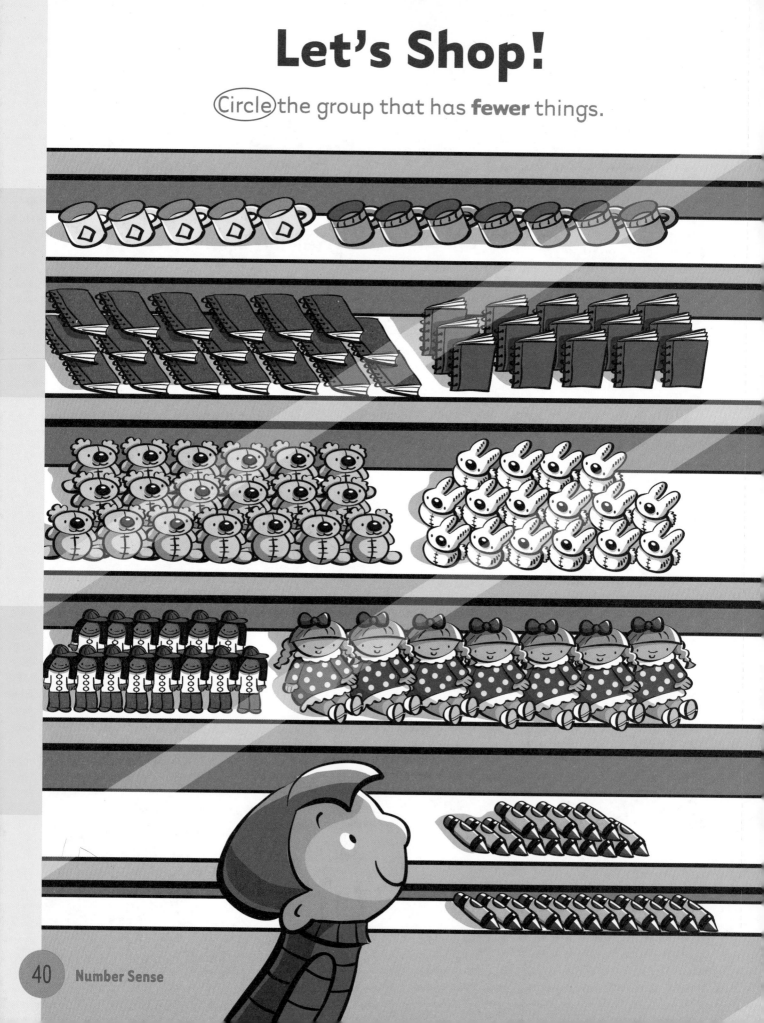

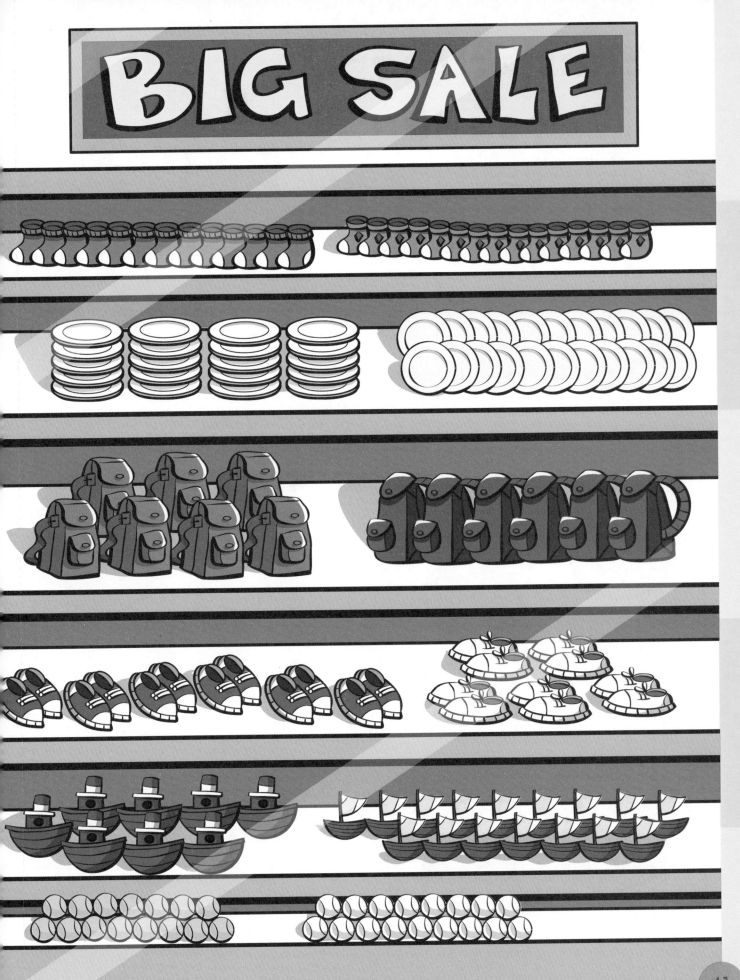

# Greater Than, Less Than

Count the polka dots on each shirt. Write the number. Draw **>**, **<**, or **=** to tell about the number pairs.

> > means "greater than": 6 > 5
> < means "less than": 5 < 6
> = means "is equal to": 5 = 5

_____

_____

_____

_____

**Number Sense**

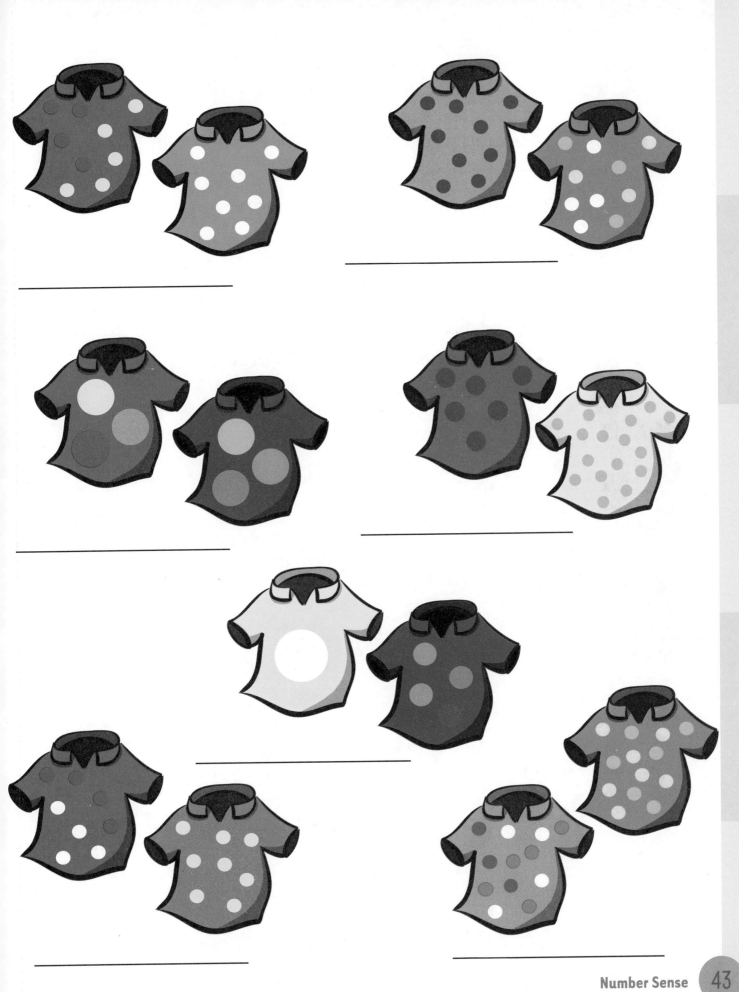

# Less Than, Greater Than

How many bowling pins do you see? Write the number on the first line. Look at the **>**, **<**, or **=** sign. Write a number that goes with that sign on the second line.

> Remember:
> \> means "greater than": 52 > 25
> < means "less than": 25 < 52
> = means "is equal to": 26 = 26

_____ < _____

_____ > _____

_____ = _____

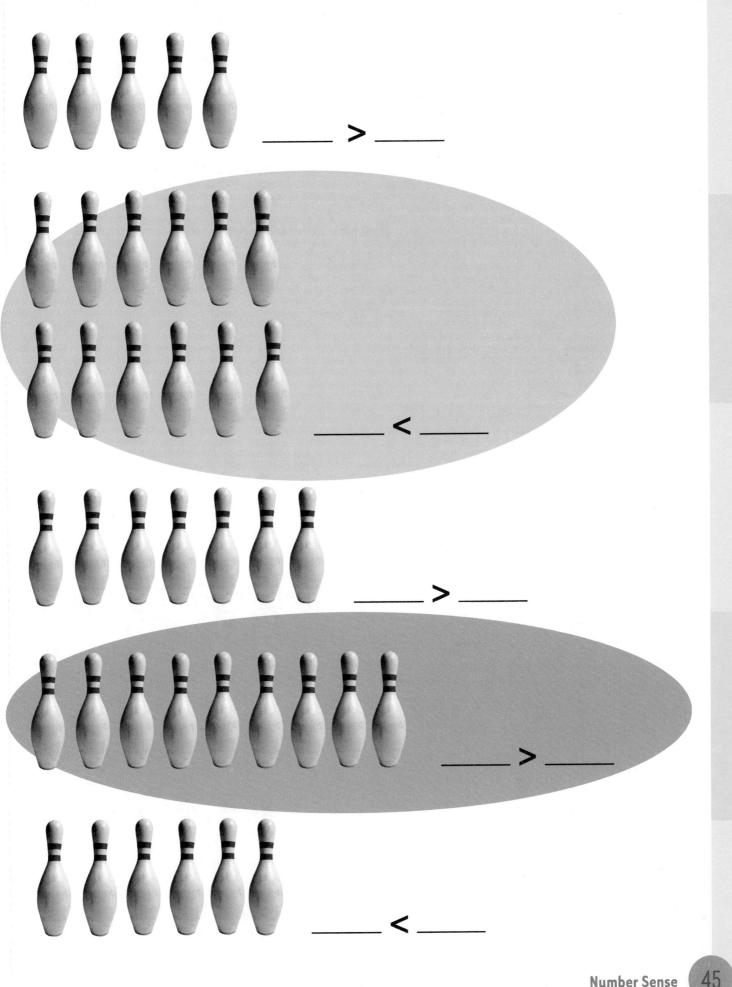

_____ > _____

_____ < _____

_____ > _____

_____ > _____

_____ < _____

# Less Than, Greater Than

Look at the number words below. Draw **>**, **<**, or **=** to tell about these word pairs.

> **Remember:**
> **>** means "greater than": 52 > 25
> **<** means "less than": 25 < 52
> **=** means "is equal to": 26 = 26

seventeen ___>___ fifteen

ten ___=___ ten

thirty ___<___ thirty-three

five ___>___ four

fifty-nine _____ fifty-one

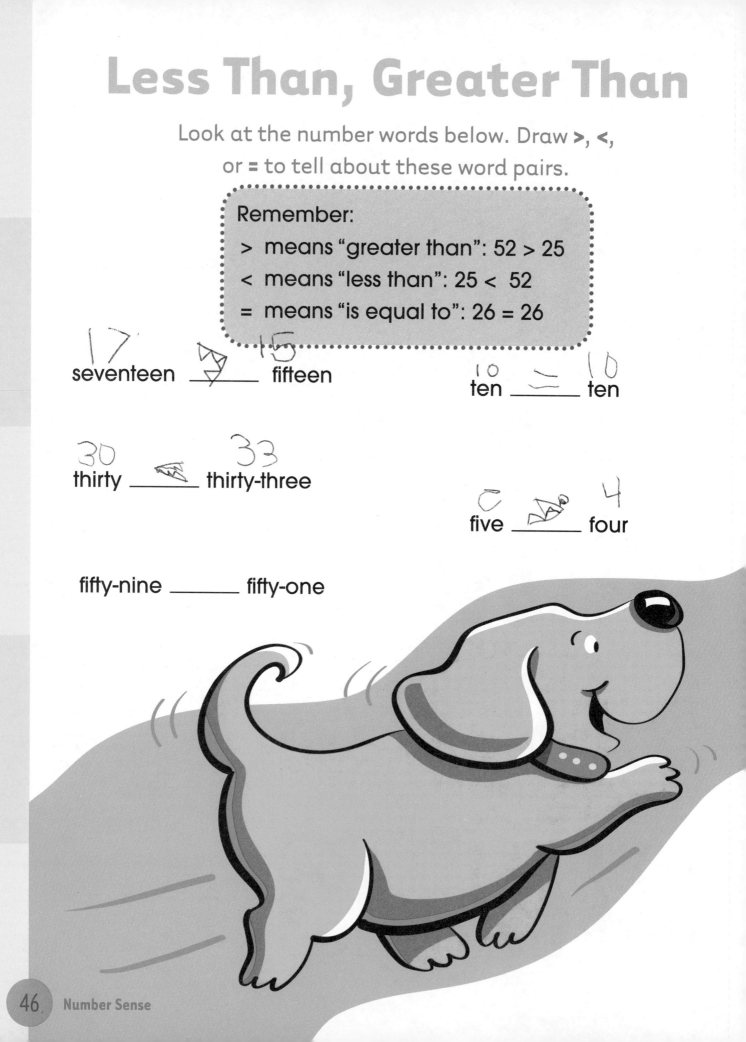

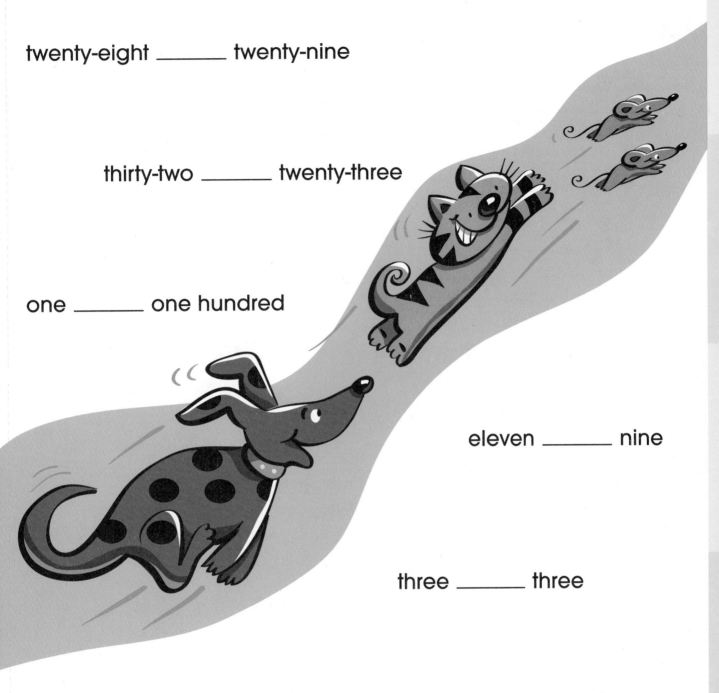

twenty-eight _____ twenty-nine

thirty-two _____ twenty-three

one _____ one hundred

eleven _____ nine

three _____ three

ninety-nine _____ one hundred

sixteen _____ sixty

# What's My Number?

My number is less than 5. It is greater than 3. What's my number?

_____

My number is greater than 6. It is less than 10. It is not 8 or 9. What's my number?

_____

My number is greater than 10. It is less than 12. It has the same number of tens and ones. What's my number?

_____

My number is greater than 14. It is less than 16. What's my number?

_____

My number comes before 1. It means "nothing." What's my number?

_____

My number is between 18 and 22. It has 2 tens and 0 ones. What's my number?

_____

My number ends in a 5. It has 3 tens. What's my number?

_____

# Number Funnies

Match each number to a word in the box.
Write the letters to find the answer to each joke.

| | | |
|---|---|---|
| two = d | seventeen = b | thirteen = j |
| nineteen = m | four = t | eighteen = p |
| three = i | fourteen = o | nine = n |
| sixteen = g | five, ten = h | seven = r |
| eleven = c | one = e | eight = f |
| six = a | twelve = u | fifteen = s |

**What do trees drink?**

_____  _____  _____  _____
  7      14     14      4

_____  _____  _____  _____!
  17      1      1       7

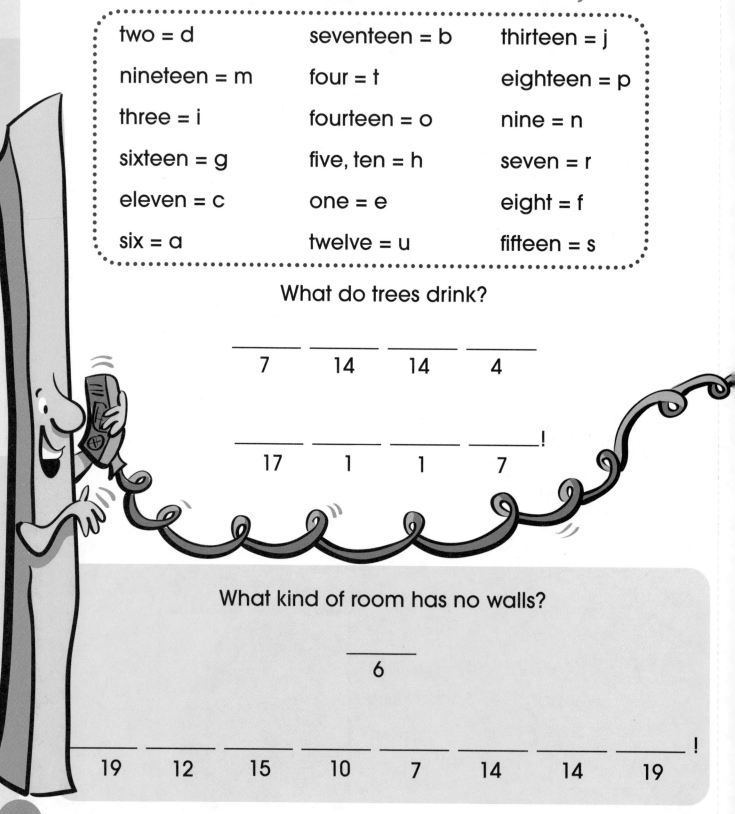

**What kind of room has no walls?**

_____
  6

_____  _____  _____  _____  _____  _____  _____  _____!
 19     12     15     10      7      14     14     19

## What did one French fry say to the other French fry?

___ ___ ___ ___ ___   ___ ___ !
11   6   4   11   5    12   18

## What do cars eat for breakfast?

___ ___ ___ ___ ___ ___ ___
4    7    6    8    8    3    11

___ ___ ___ !
13   6   19

## What kind of nut has no shell?

___
6

___ ___ ___ ___ ___ ___ ___ ___
2    14   12   16   10   9    12   4

## You have 5 apples in one hand.
## You have 7 apples in the other hand.
## What do you have?

___ ___ ___ ___ ___ ___ ___ ___ !
17   3   16   10   6    9    2    15

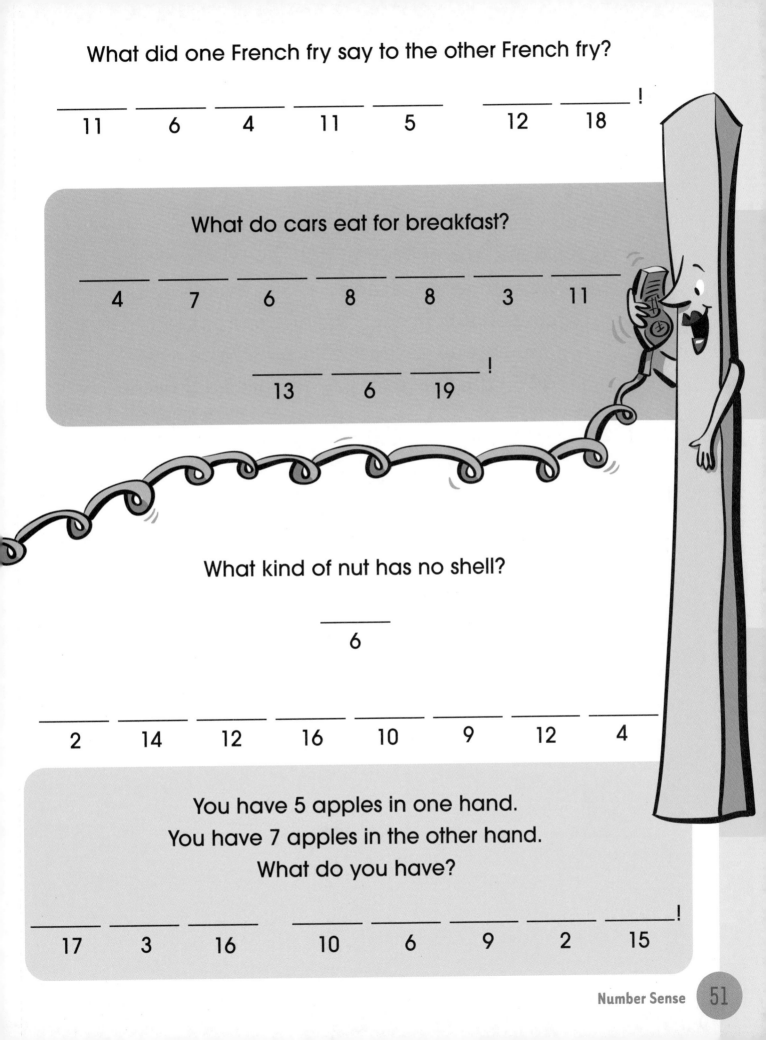

# Even and Odd

Read the number in each sentence below.
Draw that many dots, but split them into two boxes.
Hint: Go back and forth, drawing a dot in each box,
but don't put more dots in one box than in the other.
If you've drawn the number of dots and there are no dots
left over, the number you started with is **even**. If you have the
same number of dots in each box and one dot left over, the
number you started with is **odd**. Write **even**
or **odd** on the line after you've finished drawing.

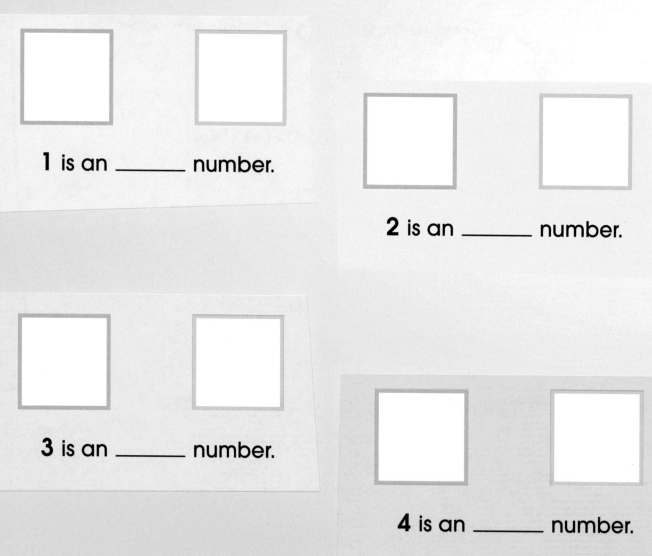

**1** is an _____ number.

**2** is an _____ number.

**3** is an _____ number.

**4** is an _____ number.

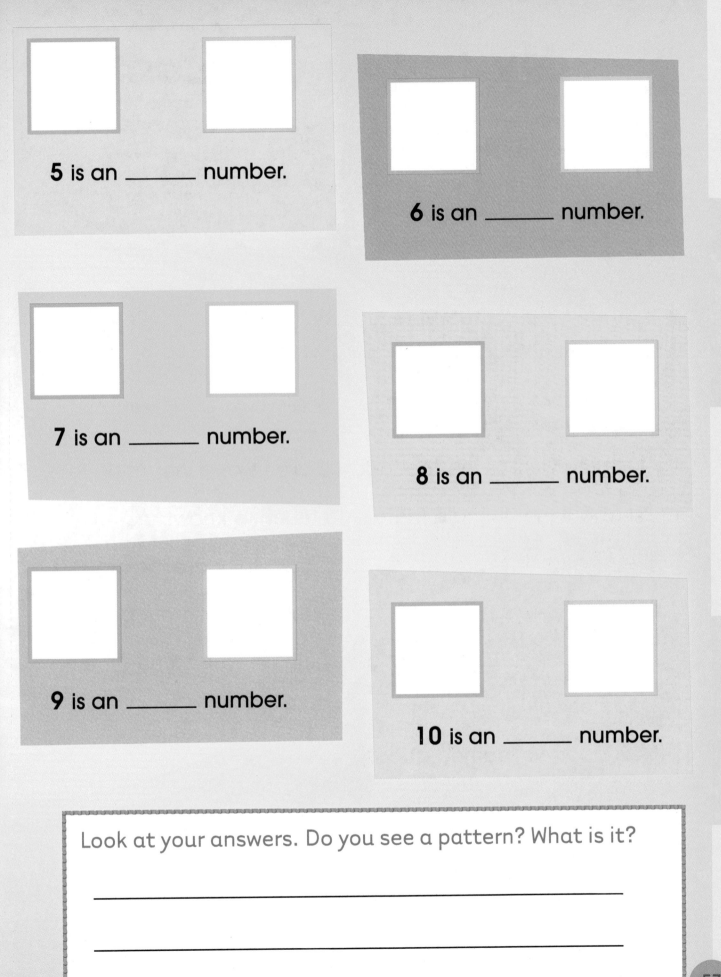

5 is an _____ number.

6 is an _____ number.

7 is an _____ number.

8 is an _____ number.

9 is an _____ number.

10 is an _____ number.

Look at your answers. Do you see a pattern? What is it?

_____

_____

# My Trip to the Zoo

The story below is missing some words. Read the clue under each line. Find the matching numbers and the missing words in the box. Write the missing words, and read the story aloud. Hint: You can use some words twice.

| | | | |
|---|---|---|---|
| 11 zebras | 90 humps | 10 camel | 59 necks |
| 8 goat | 13 brother | 23 hippo | 100 monkeys |
| 99 trunk | 41 kid | 1 stripes | 30 tigers |
| 62 cats | 80 elephant | 75 giraffes | 16 elephant's |

Our class went to the zoo today. Dr. Lee works there. She told us all about the animals. There is so much to know!

First, we saw the _____. They are the biggest
thirty

_____ on earth. They play just like our pet
sixty-two

_____ do. But one thing isn't the same—they
6 tens, 2 ones

love to get wet!

Next door, we learned about an _____
sixteen

_____. It's like a straw. An _____
ninety-nine                                    eighty

uses it to suck in water. A _____ is also like a
9 tens, 9 ones

hand. We saw one _____ use his to pick up a
8 tens, 0 ones

tiny peanut!

Then, we saw the _____s. Their name
                        2 tens, 3 ones

means "river horse." They eat grass most of the time. But Dr. Lee

said that a _____ can eat a whole lion.
                twenty-three

   We got to pet some animals, too. Guess what? A baby

_____ came up to me. It ate right out of my
        eight

hand. It's called a _____, just like me!
                        forty-one

   Have you ever seen a _____? Those
                            1 ten, 0 ones

_____ sure look funny! Watch out when a
        ninety

_____ is thirsty. Each one can drink 50 gallons
        ten

of water in one day.

   We also visited a group of _____. Their long
                                7 tens, 5 ones

_____ let them eat from tall trees. I think one
    fifty-nine

was as tall as our house!

   The _____ were cool! They all had
            eleven

_____ of black and white. Dr. Lee told us that
        one

no two _____ look alike.
        1 ten, 1 one

   Last, we saw the _____. I liked them the
                        one hundred

most. Do you know why? Two of them were playing a game of

chase. They looked just like my _____ and me!
                                    thirteen

# The Name Game

Here's a game you can play with friends and family. After you've played a few times, try changing the numbers in each sentence.

Name a food with **1** hole.

Name an animal with **2** legs.

Name a TV show that has **3** words.

Name an animal with **4** legs.

Name a word spelled with **5** letters.

Name a sport that **10** people could play.

Name someone who is more than **25** years old.

Name something that has more than **100** pieces.

# Number Sense Answer Key

*Note: Answers read across, per page.*

**4–5** 1, 2, 3, 4, 5, 6, 7, 8, 9, 10; 0

**6–7** 2, 1, 0, 6, 8, 4, 5, 10, 7, 3, 9

**8–9** Draw lines to match numbers to carrots.

**10-11** 5, 7, 0, 11, 2, 15, 6, 13, 9, 8, 1, 12, 3, 4, 10, 14; 11, 12, 13, 14, 15

**12–13** 12, 15, 11, 14, 18, 13, 19, 16, 20, 17; 11, 12, 13, 14, 15, 16, 17, 18, 19, 20

**14–15** 5, 8, 3, 13, 9, 4, 6, 13, 5,12, 14, 4

**16–17** Draw lines to connect 7/seven, 19/nineteen, 4/four, 16/sixteen, 13/thirteen, 11/eleven, 8/eight, 14/fourteen, 2/two, 20/twenty, 17/seventeen, 5/five

**18–19** Connected dots reveal a castle.

**20–21** 1–50 in sequence

**22–23** yes, no, yes, yes, no, yes, no, yes, no, yes, no, yes, yes, yes, no, no, yes, yes, no, yes, no, yes, no, no

**24–25** 1–100 in sequence

**26–27** 1; 13; 8; 24; 48; 30; 87; 52; 68; 9; 75; 20; 17, 18; 97, 98; 49, 50; 88, 89

**28–29** 2, 4, 6, 8, 10, 12, 14, 16, 18, 20

**30–31** 5, 10, 15, 20, 25, 30, 35, 40, 45, 50

**32–33** 10, 20, 30, 40, 50, 60, 70, 80, 90, 100

**34–35** 11, 17, 22, 29, 38, 35, 42, 46, 51, 58

**36–37** 2 tens, 7 ones/27; 7 tens, 8 ones/78; 3 tens, 9 ones/39; 4 tens, 1 one/41; 5 tens, 5 ones/55; 6 tens, 7 ones/67; 9 tens, 4 ones/94; 4 tens, 6 ones/46

**38–39** Circle flowers with 3, 7, 4, 11, 10, 15, 12, 14, 10, 12, 9, 15 butterflies.

**40–41** Circle 5 yellow mugs, 15 blue notebooks, 16 bunnies, 7 dolls with bows, 12 purple crayons, 13 purple socks, 22 tan plates, 6 backpacks on the right, 10 white sneakers, 8 red/blue toy boats, 15 green baseballs

**42–43** 2 < 5, 5 < 10, 7 > 4, 11 = 11, 20 > 15, 9 > 8, 9 < 10, 3 = 3, 6 < 16, 1 < 4, 8 = 8, 12 < 13

**44–45** 2, 3 or any number greater; 4, 0, 1, 2, 3; 10, 10; 5, 0, 1, 2, 3, 4; 12, 13 or any number greater; 7, 0, 1, 2, 3, 4, 5, 6; 9, 0, 1, 2, 3, 4, 5, 6, 7, 8; 6, 7 or any number greater

**46–47** >, = , < , >, > , < , > , < , >, =, <, <

**48–49** 4, 7, 11, 15, 0, 20, 35

**50–51** root beer, a mushroom, catch up, traffic jam, a doughnut, big hands

**52–53** odd, even, odd, even, odd, even, odd, even, odd, even; yes, odd and even numbers alternate.

**54–55** tigers, cats, cats, elephant's trunk, elephant, trunk, elephant, hippo, hippo, goat, kid, camel, humps, camel, giraffes, necks, zebras, stripes, zebras, monkeys, brother

# Sweet Sums

**Adding** is putting things together. The plus sign **+** tells you to add. The answer you get is called a **sum**. Add. Write the problems and the sums on the lines.

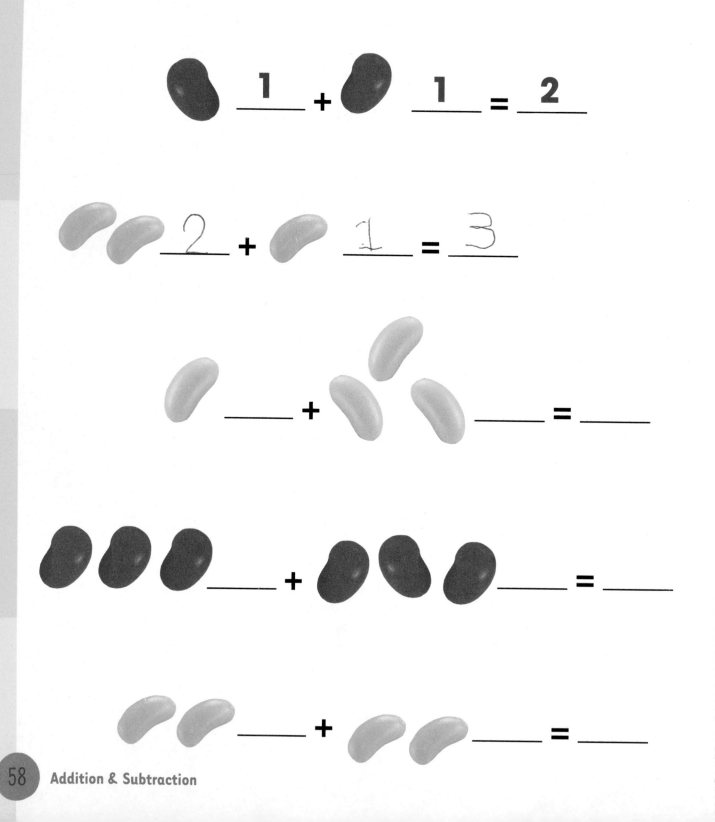

**1** + **1** = **2**

2 + 1 = 3

___ + ___ = ___

___ + ___ = ___

___ + ___ = ___

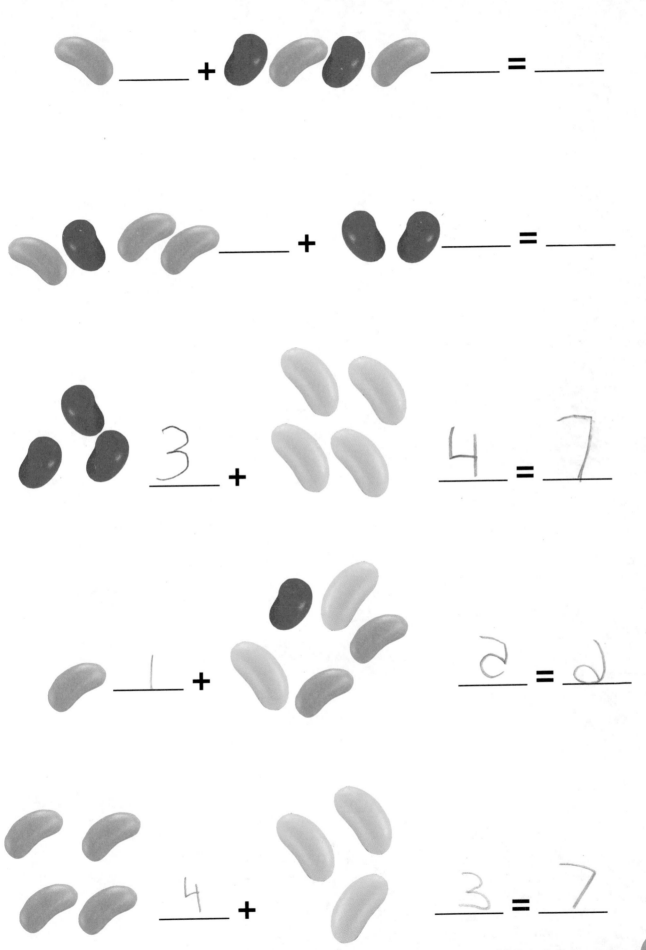

_____ + _____ = _____

_____ + _____ = _____

3 + 4 = 7

1 + 2 = 2

4 + 3 = 7

# Stars, Stars, Stars!

You can add two numbers across or up and down.
The sum will be the same! Add these numbers.
Write the sum below the line.

$$6 + 7$$

$$6 + 9$$

$$7 + 7$$

$$6 + 6$$

$$8 + 7$$

$$9 + 7$$

$$8 + 8$$

$$8 + 9$$

$$6 + 8$$

$$7 + 9$$

# How Many Cookies?

You can add numbers in any order.
The sum will be the same!

**3 + 4 = 7**

**4 + 3 = 7**

Add. Write the sum.

**5 + 7 = _____**

**8 + 9 = _____**

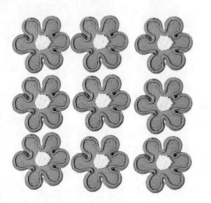

**9 + 4 = _____**

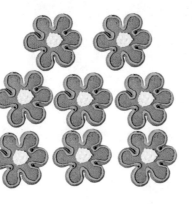

1 + 8 = _____

4 + 9 = _____

9 + 8 = _____

8 + 1 = _____

7 + 5 = _____

# In the Swim

Find the sums. Then, find the numbers in the color key, and color in each part of the picture. What do you see?

Color Key      8 = black      10 = green
11 = blue      9 = gray       12 = red

7 + 4 = _____

6 + 2 = _____

6 + 5 = _____

7 + 2 = _____

7 + 3 = _____

1 + 7 = _____

7 + 5 = _____

1 + 8 = _____

3 + 5 = _____

6 + 6 = _____

9 + 1 = _____

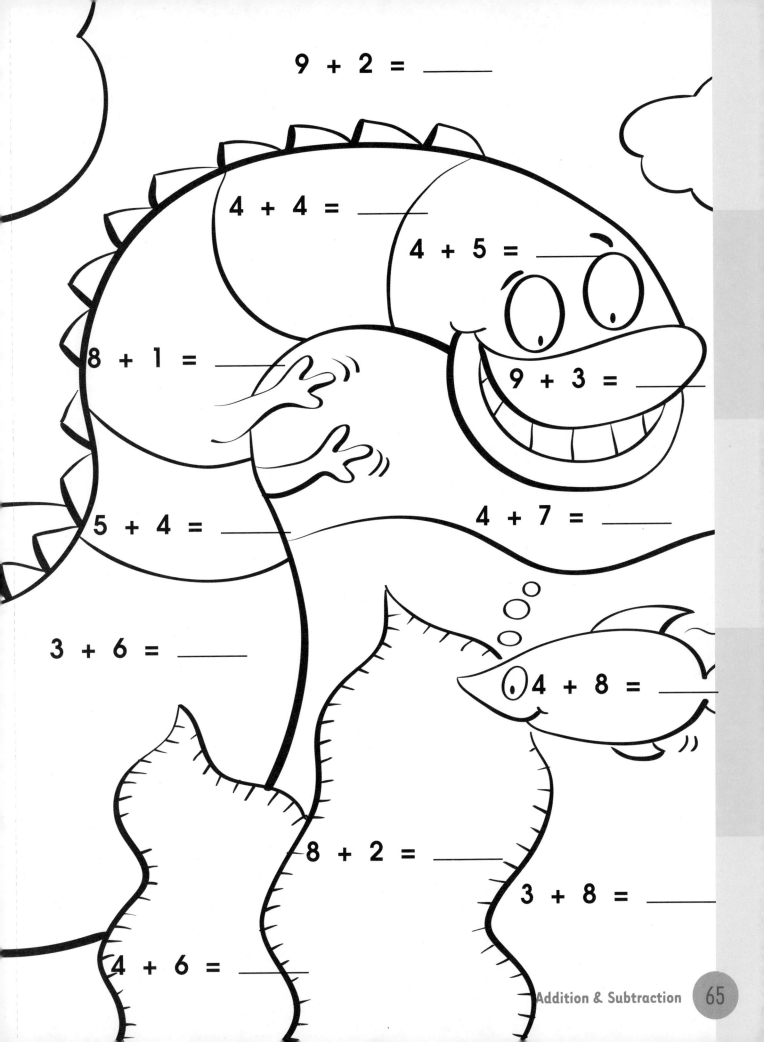

9 + 2 = _____

4 + 4 = _____

4 + 5 = _____

8 + 1 = _____

9 + 3 = _____

5 + 4 = _____

4 + 7 = _____

3 + 6 = _____

4 + 8 = _____

8 + 2 = _____

3 + 8 = _____

4 + 6 = _____

# Bears Add Up

Add. Write the sums.

|  |  |  |  |
|---|---|---|---|
| 14<br>+ 2 | 10<br>+ 9 | 15<br>+ 2 | 11<br>+ 5 |
| 12<br>+ 3 | 13<br>+ 1 | 17<br>+ 2 | 11<br>+ 4 |
| 10<br>+ 1 | 11<br>+ 7 | 13<br>+ 5 | 12<br>+ 7 |

Addition & Subtraction

```
  15          13          11          10
 + 1         + 3         + 2         + 5
-----       -----       -----       -----


  12          13          11          10
 + 2         + 4         + 3         + 6
-----       -----       -----       -----


  12          13          12          10
 + 5         + 2         + 4         + 3
-----       -----       -----       -----


  14          16          10          16
 + 4         + 3         + 7         + 2
-----       -----       -----       -----


  14          17          10          15
 + 3         + 1         + 2         + 3
-----       -----       -----       -----
```

# Big-Top Sums

Add. Write the sums.

| | | | |
|---|---|---|---|
| 15<br>+ 2 | 17<br>+ 2 | 15<br>+ 1 | 12<br>+ 2 |
| 14<br>+ 3 | 11<br>+ 4 | 14<br>+ 2 | 10<br>+ 2 |
| 12<br>+ 3 | 10<br>+ 1 | 11<br>+ 2 | 13<br>+ 4 |
| 15<br>+ 3 | 13<br>+ 5 | 10<br>+ 5 | 11<br>+ 3 |

$$10 \atop + 6$$

$$10 \atop + 3$$

$$13 \atop + 2$$

$$10 \atop + 9$$

$$11 \atop + 5$$

$$16 \atop + 3$$

$$12 \atop + 4$$

$$10 \atop + 7$$

# Fruit and More Fruit

Write out the problem below the pictures.

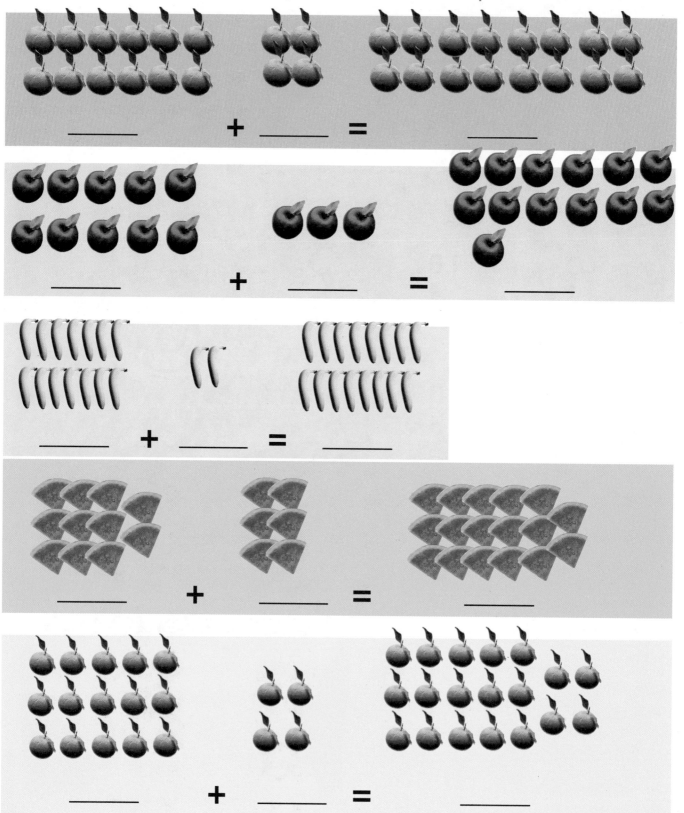

_____ + _____ = _____

_____ + _____ = _____

_____ + _____ = _____

_____ + _____ = _____

_____ + _____ = _____

_____ + _____ = _____

_____ + _____ = _____

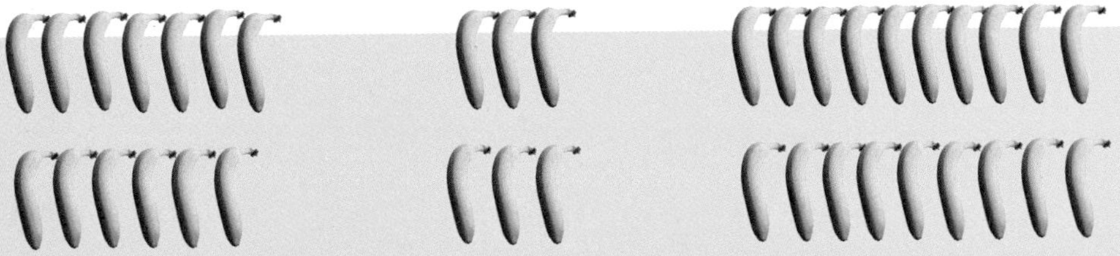

_____ + _____ = _____

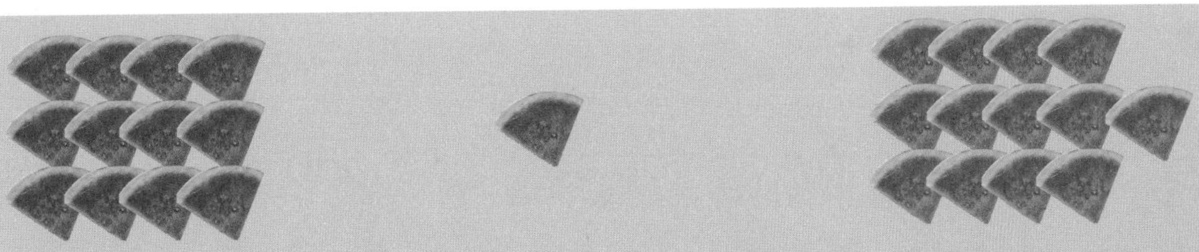

_____ + _____ = _____

_____ + _____ = _____

_____ + _____ = _____

# Jungle Jokes

Match each problem to a sum in the box.
Fill in the letters to find the answer to each joke.

**Letter Code**

| | | | | |
|---|---|---|---|---|
| 11 = m | 10 = a | 18 = t | 19 = u | 6 = l | 4 = c |
| 16 = i | 3 = p | 14 = h | 7 = n | 13 = o | 5 = k |
| 9 = r | 17 = f | 12 = e | 8 = b | 15 = s | |

## What time is it when you see a tiger?

\_\_\_\_ \_\_\_\_ \_\_\_\_ \_\_\_\_
12 + 6  13 + 3  5 + 6  9 + 3

\_\_\_\_ \_\_\_\_   \_\_\_\_ \_\_\_\_ \_\_\_\_!
14 + 4  7 + 6   5 + 4  15 + 4  3 + 4

## How do you catch a monkey?

\_\_\_\_ \_\_\_\_ \_\_\_\_
9 + 1  3 + 1  15 + 3

\_\_\_\_ \_\_\_\_ \_\_\_\_ \_\_\_\_  \_\_\_\_
5 + 1  12 + 4  1 + 4  8 + 4  10 + 0

\_\_\_\_ \_\_\_\_ \_\_\_\_ \_\_\_\_ \_\_\_\_ \_\_\_\_!
4 + 4  5 + 5  1 + 6  9 + 1  7 + 0  1 + 9

How many coconuts grow
on trees?

___ ___ ___
5 + 5  4 + 2  5 + 1

___ ___
10 + 3  2 + 15

___ ___ ___ ___!
9 + 9  8 + 6  7 + 5  10 + 1

What kind of trees can clap?

___ ___ ___ ___
1 + 2  6 + 4  2 + 4  3 + 8

___ ___ ___ ___ ___!
13 + 5  3 + 6  10 + 2  4 + 8  7 + 8

What did one banana say to the other?

___ ___ ___ ___ ___ ___
17 + 1  9 + 5  7 + 3  1 + 6  4 + 1  9 + 6

___ ___ ___ ___ ___ ___!
8 + 2  3 + 5  16 + 3  5 + 2  2 + 2  10 + 4

# Subtract the Shells

**Subtraction** is taking things away. The minus sign — tells you to subtract. The answer you get is the **difference**.

Subtract. Write the problems and the differences on the line.

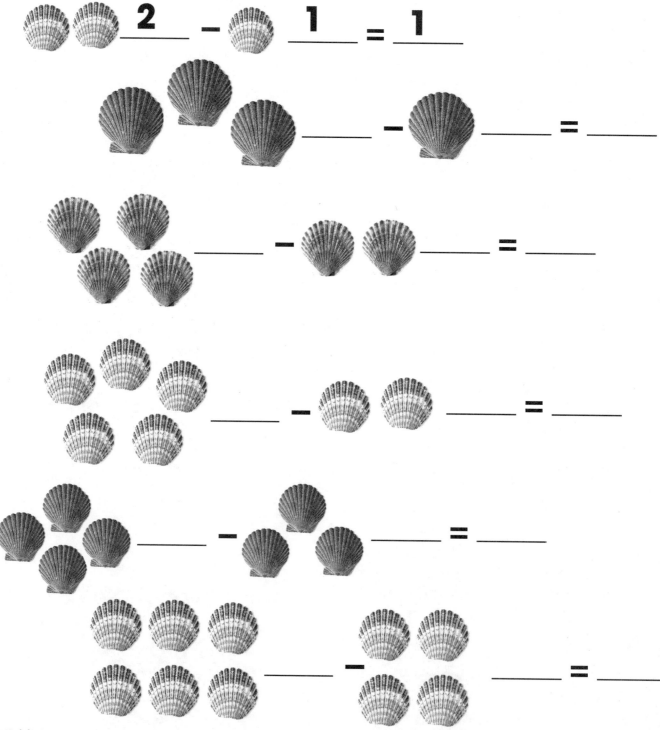

**2** — **1** = **1**

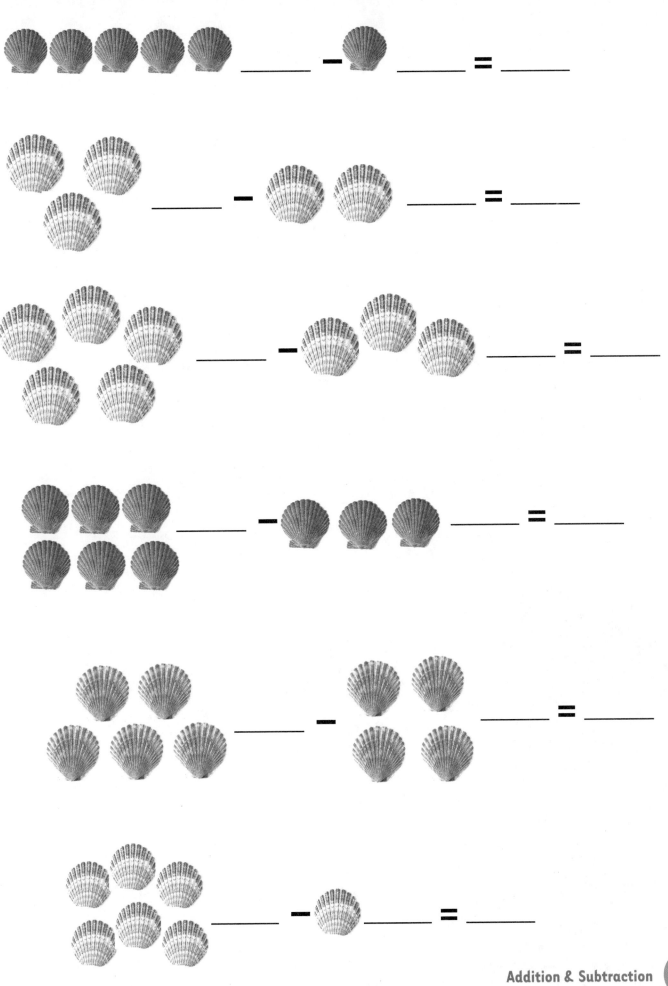

_____ – _____ = _____

_____ – _____ = _____

_____ – _____ = _____

_____ – _____ = _____

_____ – _____ = _____

_____ – _____ = _____

# Subtraction Magic

Subtract. Write the problems and the difference on the lines.

_____ - _____ = _____

_____ - _____ = _____

_____ - _____ = _____

_____ - _____ = _____

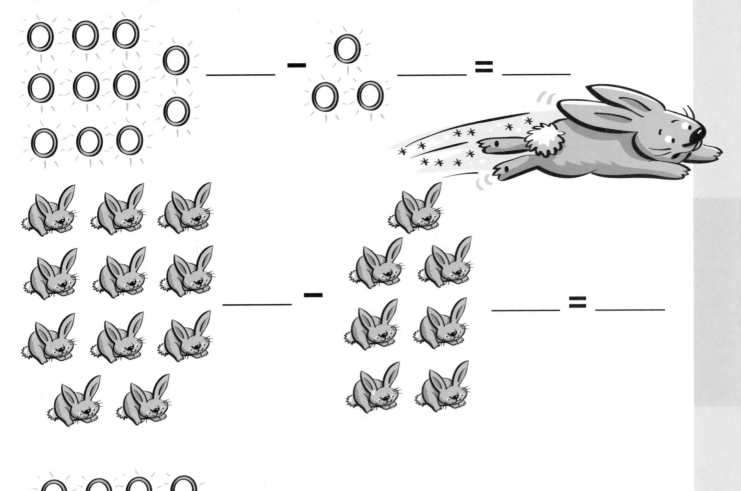

_____ - _____ = _____

_____ - _____ = _____

_____ - _____ = _____

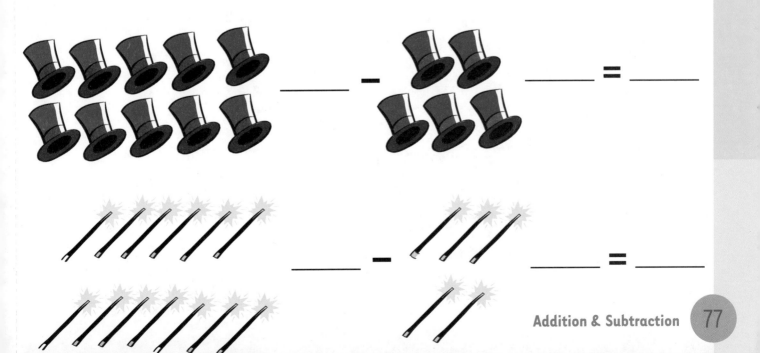

_____ - _____ = _____

_____ - _____ = _____

# Dino Differences

Subtract. Write the difference on the line.

$15 - 6 =$ _____        $13 - 7 =$ _____

$12 - 9 =$ _____        $11 - 4 =$ _____

$15 - 2 =$ _____        $13 - 5 =$ _____

$10 - 6 =$ _____        $10 - 10 =$ _____

$11 - 2 =$ _____        $16 - 8 =$ _____

$10 - 5 =$ _____        $12 - 2 =$ _____

$14 - 5 =$ _____        $14 - 3 =$ _____

12 – 3 = _____

17 – 2 = _____

10 – 6 = _____

13 – 8 = _____

11 – 3 = _____

15 – 8 = _____

# Fact Families

You can use addition to check a subtraction sentence. Here's how: Subtract first, and find the difference. Write the difference in the addition sentence. Find the sum. The sum will be the first number in the subtraction sentence!

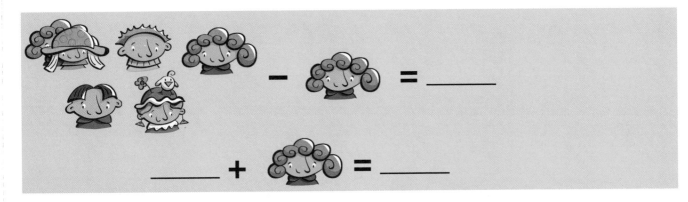

# Addition or Subtraction?

Read each math sentence.
Write + or — to complete the sentence.

12
6
___
6

13
5
___
8

10
2
___
12

15
6
___
9

12
9
___
3

15
2
___
17

8
3
___
11

14
2
___
12

11
5
___
16

| | | |
|---|---|---|
| 10<br>5<br>——<br>5 | 12<br>2<br>——<br>10 | 14<br>3<br>——<br>17 |
| 12<br>3<br>——<br>9 | 17<br>2<br>——<br>19 | 11<br>4<br>——<br>15 |
| 15<br>5<br>——<br>10 | 12<br>7<br>——<br>5 | 11<br>6<br>——<br>17 |
| 10<br>4<br>——<br>14 | 15<br>8<br>——<br>7 | 16<br>8<br>——<br>8 |
| 10<br>3<br>——<br>13 | 14<br>4<br>——<br>18 | 5<br>8<br>——<br>13 |

# Monkey Business

Is the problem true or false?
<u>Underline</u> the monkey that has the correct answer.

$15 + 2 = 17$

true          false

$11 - 3 = 10$

true          false

$13 - 4 = 9$

true          false

$14 + 5 = 17$

true          false

$10 - 2 = 7$

true          false

$16 + 1 = 17$

true          false

$14 + 4 = 19$

true    false

$13 - 3 = 10$

true    false

$10 + 2 = 12$

true    false

$12 - 4 = 9$

true    false

$15 + 3 = 18$

true    false

$17 - 7 = 8$

true    false

# Math Buzz

Add or subtract. Then bring the bees home to their hive. Match each picture problem to a number problem.

Addition & Subtraction

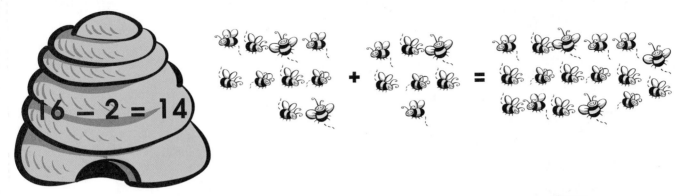

16 − 2 = 14

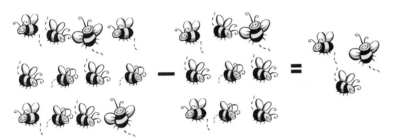

12 + 2 = 14

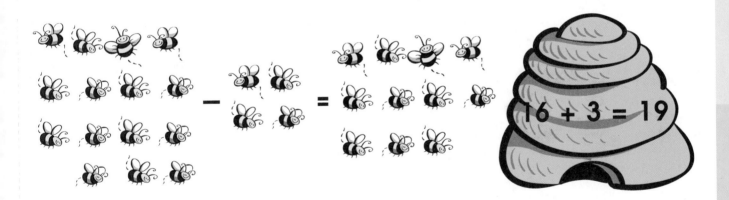

16 + 3 = 19

13 + 5 = 18

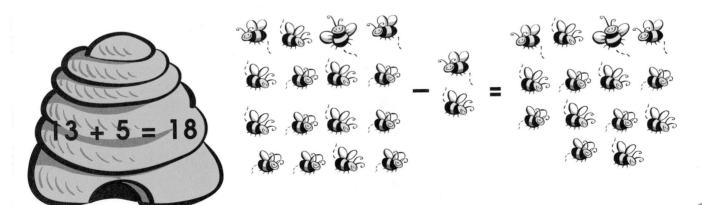

# Give the Dogs a Bone

Add or subtract. Match each dog to a bone.

1 + 2

9 − 6

4 + 1

7 − 2

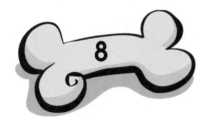

3 + 3

8 − 2

6

1 + 1
6 − 4

2 + 2
7 − 3

3

5

5 + 3
9 − 1

# All Sewn Up

Write the number problem below the pictures.

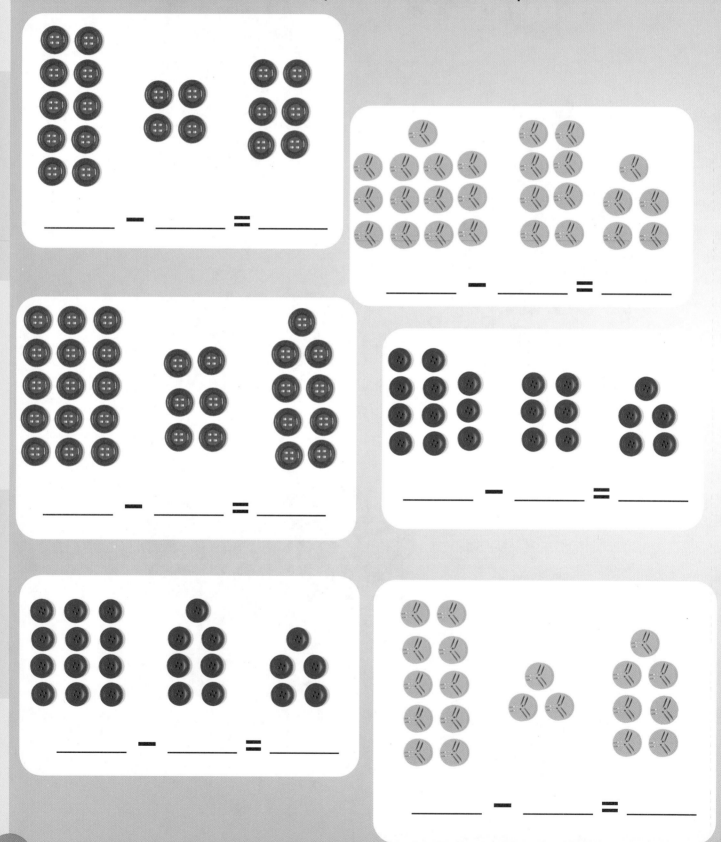

_____ − _____ = _____

_____ − _____ = _____

_____ − _____ = _____

_____ − _____ = _____

_____ − _____ = _____

_____ − _____ = _____

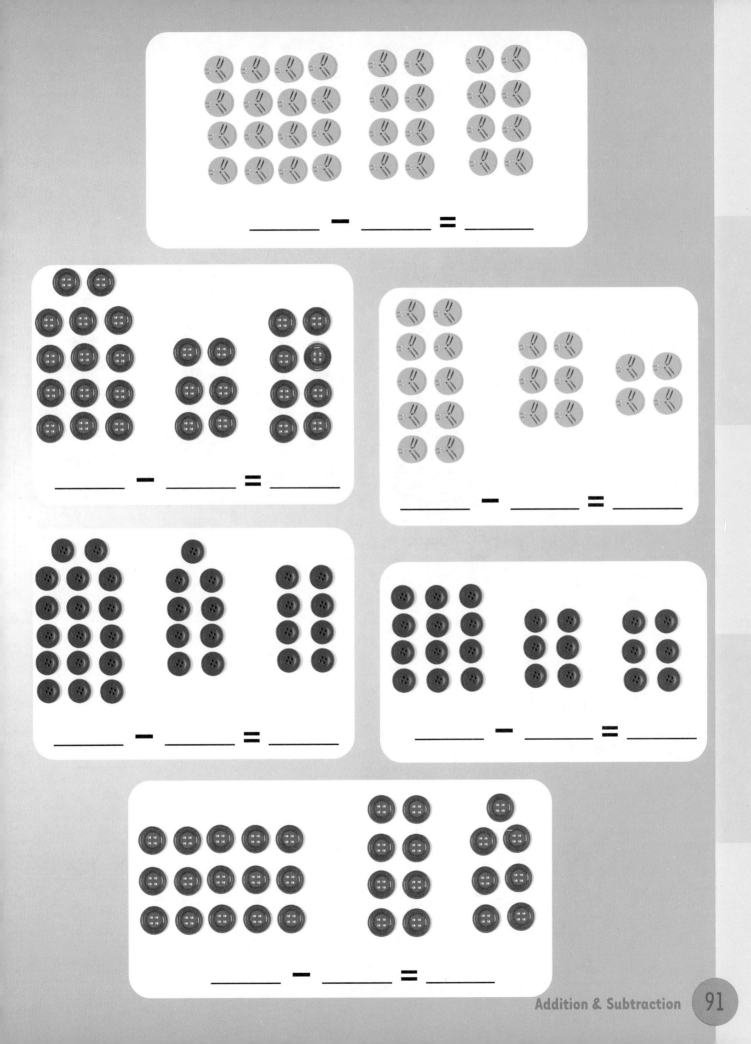

_____ - _____ = _____

_____ - _____ = _____

_____ - _____ = _____

_____ - _____ = _____

_____ - _____ = _____

_____ - _____ = _____

# Catch a Math Wave!

Add or subtract.

```
  14          13          10
+  5        -  8        +  6
————        ————        ————
```

```
  12                      12
+  5                    +  6
————                    ————
```

15
− 6
_____

10
+ 4
_____

12
+ 7
_____

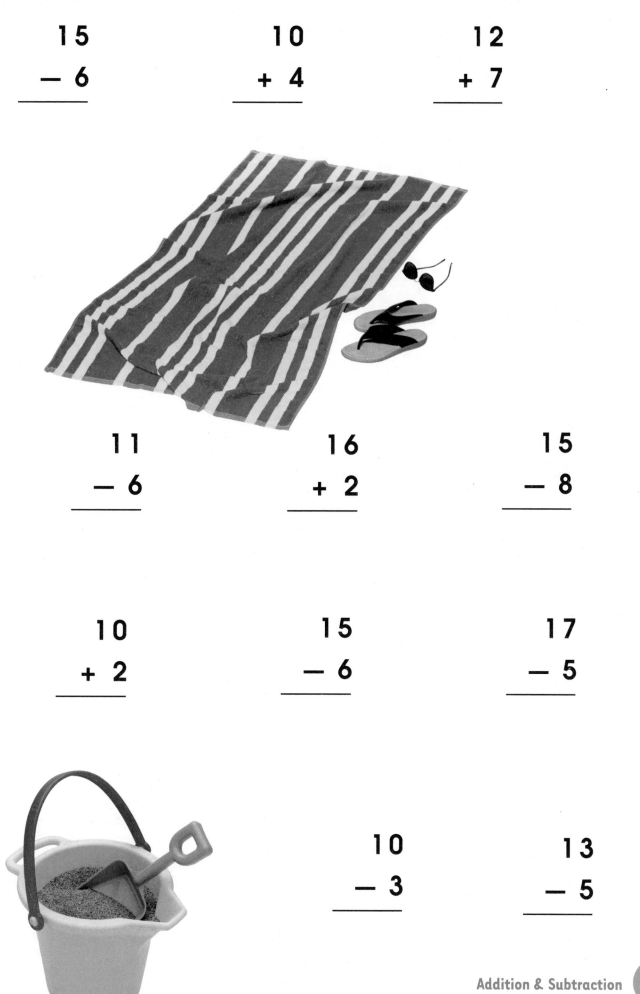

11
− 6
_____

16
+ 2
_____

15
− 8
_____

10
+ 2
_____

15
− 6
_____

17
− 5
_____

10
− 3
_____

13
− 5
_____

# X Marks the Spot

14
+ 3
___

16
− 6
___

10
+ 2
___

10
+ 5
___
15

13
+ 2
___
15

15
− 4
___

19
− 4
___
15

9
+ 7
___

11
+ 3
___

15
+ 0
___
15

17
+ 2
___

14
− 2
___

11
+ 4
___
15

**Start**

Add or subtract. Follow the trail to the X over the hidden treasure. It goes through all the problems whose answer is **15**.

$$\begin{array}{r} 15 \\ -\ 0 \\ \hline 15 \end{array}$$

$$\begin{array}{r} 9 \\ +\ 6 \\ \hline 15 \end{array}$$

$$\begin{array}{r} 15 \\ -\ 2 \\ \hline \end{array}$$

$$\begin{array}{r} 12 \\ +\ 3 \\ \hline 15 \end{array}$$

$$\begin{array}{r} 10 \\ +\ 4 \\ \hline \end{array}$$

$$\begin{array}{r} 18 \\ -\ 3 \\ \hline 15 \end{array}$$

$$\begin{array}{r} 14 \\ +\ 0 \\ \hline \end{array}$$

$$\begin{array}{r} 9 \\ +\ 5 \\ \hline \end{array}$$

$$\begin{array}{r} 14 \\ +\ 1 \\ \hline 15 \end{array}$$

$$\begin{array}{r} 16 \\ -\ 3 \\ \hline \end{array}$$

$$\begin{array}{r} 14 \\ +\ 2 \\ \hline \end{array}$$

$$\begin{array}{r} 17 \\ -\ 2 \\ \hline 15 \end{array}$$

$$\begin{array}{r} 9 \\ +\ 3 \\ \hline \end{array}$$

$$\begin{array}{r} 17 \\ -\ 3 \\ \hline \end{array}$$

$$\begin{array}{r} 8 \\ +\ 7 \\ \hline 15 \end{array}$$

$$\begin{array}{r} 17 \\ +\ 2 \\ \hline \end{array}$$

$$\begin{array}{r} 16 \\ -\ 1 \\ \hline 15 \end{array}$$

# Goal!

Read about the Rose City soccer team. If you need to, draw pictures to help solve each problem. Add or subtract to find the answers.

**1.** Maria scored five goals this week. _____

She scored three goals last week. +_____

How many goals in two weeks? _____

**2.** The team has fifteen players. _____

Eleven players can be on the field. — _____

How many players must sit out? _____

**3.** The team has twelve games this month. _____

The team has six games next month. +_____

How many games in two months? _____

**4.** The team has ten soccer balls. _____

Coach Wood bought seven more balls. + _____

How many balls does the team have? _____

**5.** Kisha's dad made thirteen sandwiches for the team. _____

The players ate nine sandwiches. − _____

How many sandwiches were left? _____

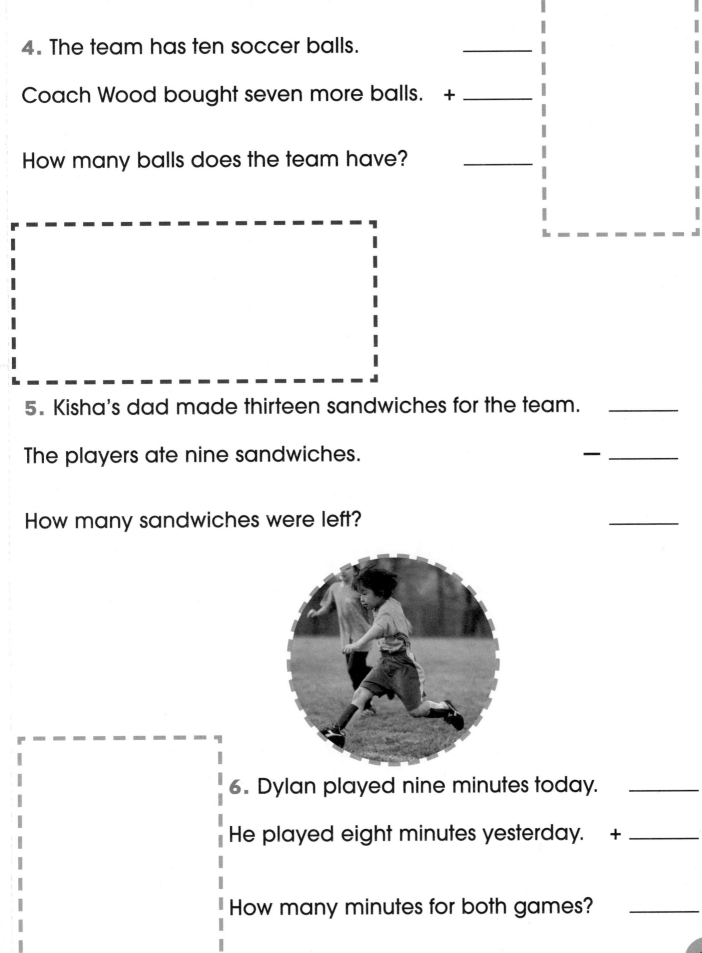

**6.** Dylan played nine minutes today. _____

He played eight minutes yesterday. + _____

How many minutes for both games? _____

# Ahoy, Math Mate!

Read the problem on each boat.
Color in the sail with the answer.

9    7

one **more** than 8

3    1

one **less** than 2

10    8

one **less** than 9

6    8

one **more** than 7

13    11

one **more** than 12

13    15

one **more** than 14

6    4

one **less** than 5

12  14

one **less** than 13

9  11

one **more** than 10

7  5

one **less** than 6

16  18

one **more** than 17

10  12

one **less** than 11

17  19

one **more** than 18

2  0

one **less** than 1

4  2

one **less** than 3

16  14

one **more** than 15

# 1, 2, 3 . . . Add!

Draw balloons next to each number. Add.
Write the sum below the line.

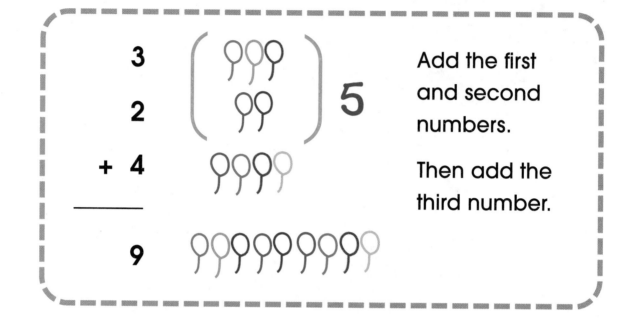

Add the first
and second
numbers.

Then add the
third number.

| | | | 4 |
| | | | 2 |
| + | 1 | | + 1 |

```
    5              9        ⟨9⟩ 98
    6              1
  + 7            + 2
  ─────          ─────      9
                   12
```

```
    7              6
    1              4
  + 7            + 2
  ─────          ─────
```

```
    3              2
    5              4
  + 6            + 7
  ─────          ─────
```

# Add It Up

Add the first and second numbers.
Then add the third number.

```
  3  ⎫
  1  ⎬ 4
+ 2  ⎭
____
  6
```

Add. See the box if you need help.

```
   2          3          4          7
   4          0          2          3
+  6       +  9       +  3       +  6
____       ____       ____       ____
```

```
   2          6          9          1
   1          2          5          8
+  2       +  0       +  3       +  2
____       ____       ____       ____
```

```
    4              2              4              7
    7              2              1              4
  + 3            + 2            + 0            + 4
  ─────          ─────          ─────          ─────


    2              0              1              2
    6              9              1              5
  + 6            + 3            + 7            + 5
  ─────          ─────          ─────          ─────


    1              3              7              5
    3              6              7              9
  + 4            + 1            + 7            + 0
  ─────          ─────          ─────          ─────
```

# What a Picnic!

Read the story. Answer the questions.

Last week, my family went on a picnic. We have seven people in our family. Aunt Karen's family went along. My aunt has five people in her family.

How many people went on the picnic?

\_\_\_\_\_ people **+** \_\_\_\_\_ people **=** \_\_\_\_\_ people

We all got in our van. We drove ten miles to a gas station. We put gas in the van. Then, we drove five more miles to the picnic area.

How many miles did we drive?

\_\_\_\_\_ miles **+** \_\_\_\_\_ miles **=** \_\_\_\_\_ miles

Dad set down a blanket. He looked at us.

"Kids, we'll need wood for the fire. Can you get it?"

Off we went. I found four logs. My brother found five logs. Cousin Sarah had the most. She found seven logs!

How many logs did the kids find?

\_\_\_\_\_ logs **+** \_\_\_\_\_ logs **+** \_\_\_\_\_ logs **=** \_\_\_\_\_ logs

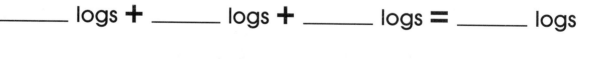

Mom looked into the picnic basket.

"Oh, no!" said Mom.

"What is it, Mom?" asked my sister.

"I had twelve plates at home. But I only brought five!"

How many plates did Mom leave at home?

_____ plates $-$ _____ plates $=$ _____ plates

"That's okay," said Uncle Jeff. "We have lots of food. We brought sixteen hot dogs."

Cousin Sarah looked into the picnic basket.

"Uh-oh," said Sarah. "We only have nine buns!"

How many more hot dogs than buns?

_____ hot dogs $-$ _____ buns $=$ _____ hot dogs

"At least we have soda to drink," said Dad. "We have nine cans."

Uncle Jeff gave a loud laugh. "We have nine cans, too! So much soda!"

How many cans of soda at the picnic?

_____ cans $+$ _____ cans $=$ _____ cans

Aunt Karen spoke. "I have a surprise. I made twelve little cakes. They will taste good after lunch."

Mom looked into the picnic basket.

"Guess what?" asked Mom. "We have twelve forks!"

We all had a laugh. The right number at last! What a picnic!

# Handy Tens

Add the **10s**. Look at the box if you need help.

**Adding Tens**

$$10$$
$$+ 20$$
$$\overline{\phantom{0}}$$
$$30$$ ———— Put a **0** in the **ones** place.

— **Add** the numbers in the **tens** place.

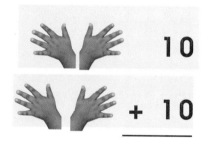

$$10$$
$$+ 10$$
$$\overline{\phantom{0}}$$

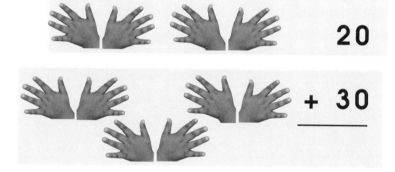

$$20$$

$$+ 30$$
$$\overline{\phantom{0}}$$

$$10$$
$$+ 40$$
$$\overline{\phantom{0}}$$

$$20$$
$$+ 20$$
$$\overline{\phantom{0}}$$

$$40$$
$$+ 30$$
$$\overline{\phantom{0}}$$

```
  50          60          20
+ 20        + 10        + 70
____        ____        ____


  10          30          10
+ 30        + 30        + 50
____        ____        ____


  50          10          20
+ 30        + 60        + 60
____        ____        ____


  10          40          70
+ 80        + 20        + 10
____        ____        ____


  30          40          50
+ 60        + 40        + 40
____        ____        ____
```

# Tens on the Loose

Subtract the **tens**. Look at the box if you need help.

**Subracting Tens**

```
   30
 − 10
 ————
   20 ——————— Put a 0 in the ones place.
          └——— Subtract the numbers in
               the tens place.
```

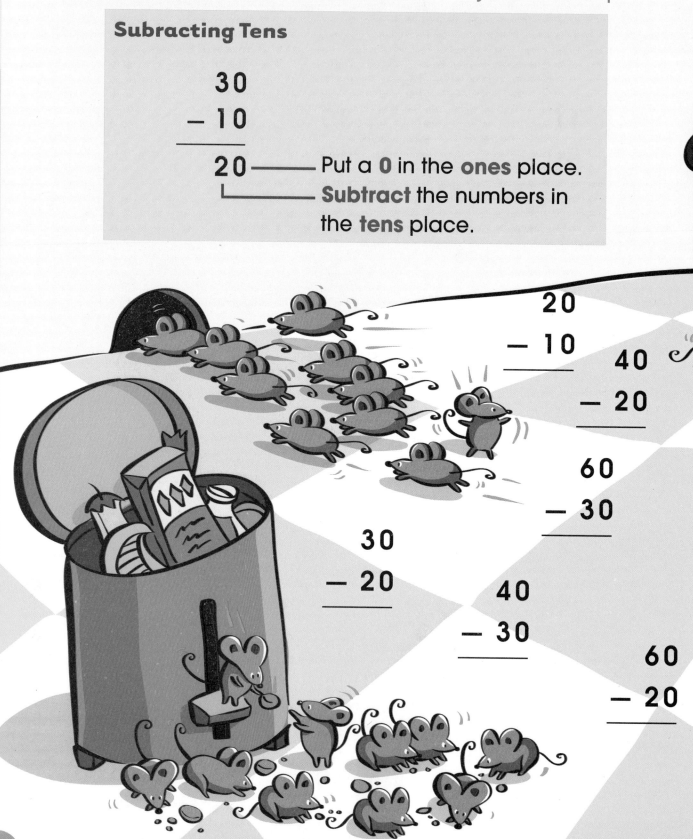

```
   20
 − 10
 ————
```

```
   40
 − 20
 ————
```

```
   60
 − 30
 ————
```

```
   30
 − 20
 ————
```

```
   40
 − 30
 ————
```

```
   60
 − 20
 ————
```

$$\begin{array}{r} 50 \\ -\ 30 \\ \hline \end{array}$$

$$\begin{array}{r} 70 \\ -\ 20 \\ \hline \end{array}$$

$$\begin{array}{r} 50 \\ -\ 20 \\ \hline \end{array}$$

$$\begin{array}{r} 70 \\ -\ 40 \\ \hline \end{array}$$

$$\begin{array}{r} 80 \\ -\ 40 \\ \hline \end{array}$$

$$\begin{array}{r} 60 \\ -\ 40 \\ \hline \end{array}$$

$$\begin{array}{r} 50 \\ -\ 10 \\ \hline \end{array}$$

$$\begin{array}{r} 90 \\ -\ 30 \\ \hline \end{array}$$

$$\begin{array}{r} 50 \\ -\ 40 \\ \hline \end{array}$$

# What's My Number?

Write the number on the line.

My number is 10 more than 40.
What's my number?

_____

My number is 10 less than 20.
What's my number?

_____

My number is 10 more than 30.
What's my number?

_____

My number is 10 less than 40.
What's my number?

_____

My number is 10 more than 10.
What's my number?

_____

My number is 10 less than 90.
What's my number?

_____

My number is 10 more than 70.
What's my number?

_____

My number is 10 less than 50.
What's my number?

_____

My number is 10 more than 60.
What's my number?

_____

My number is 10 less than 80.
What's my number?

_____

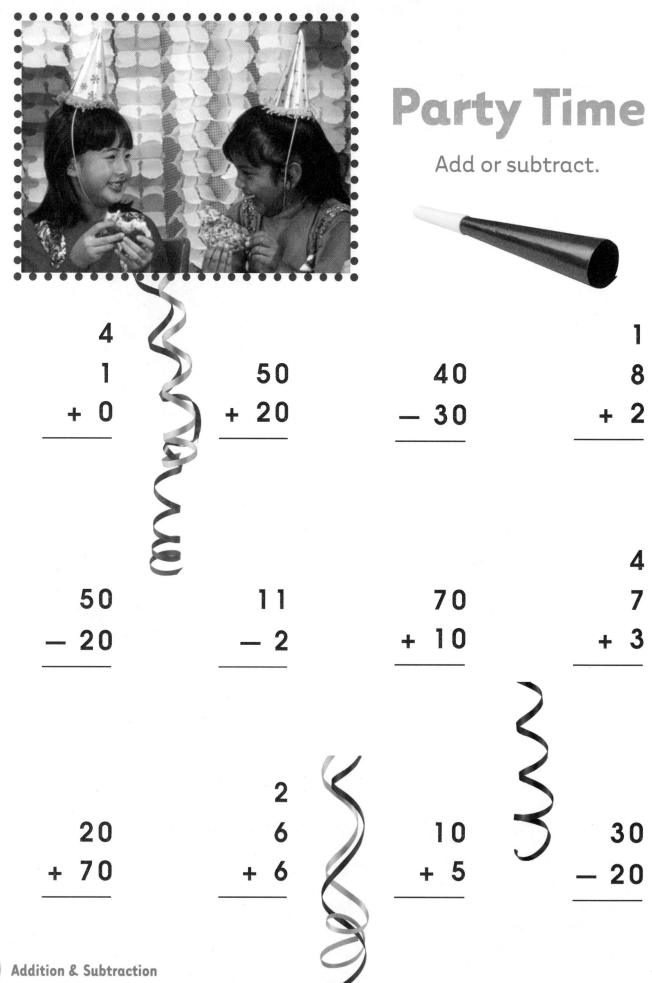

# Party Time

Add or subtract.

```
    4
    1          50          40           1
+   0        + 20        – 30           8
_____     _____    _____     + 2
                                      _____


   50          11          70           4
 – 20         – 2        + 10           7
_____     _____    _____     + 3
                                      _____


   20           2          10          30
 + 70           6        +  5        – 20
_____        6        _____    _____
              + 6
             _____
```

$$\begin{array}{r} 11 \\ + \ 4 \\ \hline \end{array} \qquad \begin{array}{r} 7 \\ 4 \\ + \ 4 \\ \hline \end{array} \qquad \begin{array}{r} 15 \\ - \ 1 \\ \hline \end{array} \qquad \begin{array}{r} 15 \\ + \ 2 \\ \hline \end{array}$$

$$\begin{array}{r} 40 \\ + \ 30 \\ \hline \end{array} \qquad \begin{array}{r} 13 \\ - \ 4 \\ \hline \end{array} \qquad \begin{array}{r} 60 \\ - \ 30 \\ \hline \end{array} \qquad \begin{array}{r} 70 \\ - \ 40 \\ \hline \end{array}$$

$$\begin{array}{r} 13 \\ + \ 5 \\ \hline \end{array} \qquad \begin{array}{r} 50 \\ - \ 30 \\ \hline \end{array} \qquad \begin{array}{r} 4 \\ 8 \\ + \ 8 \\ \hline \end{array} \qquad \begin{array}{r} 12 \\ - \ 9 \\ \hline \end{array}$$

$$\begin{array}{r} 20 \\ - \ 10 \\ \hline \end{array} \qquad \begin{array}{r} 20 \\ + \ 20 \\ \hline \end{array} \qquad \begin{array}{r} 2 \\ 2 \\ + \ 2 \\ \hline \end{array} \qquad \begin{array}{r} 20 \\ + \ 30 \\ \hline \end{array}$$

$$\begin{array}{r} 10 \\ + \ 40 \\ \hline \end{array} \qquad \begin{array}{r} 40 \\ - \ 20 \\ \hline \end{array} \qquad \begin{array}{r} 3 \\ 3 \\ + \ 0 \\ \hline \end{array} \qquad \begin{array}{r} 60 \\ + \ 10 \\ \hline \end{array}$$

# Math Magic

Here is a fun math trick. Try it out.
Then try it on a friend!

**Step 1.** Pick a number.

**Step 2.** Add **9** to the answer.          + 9 _____

**Step 3.** Subtract **6** from the answer.   − 6 _____

**Step 4.** Add **2** to your answer.         + 2 _____

**Step 5.** Subtract your first number
from the answer.                    − ◯

Your answer will always be **5**!

# Addition & Subtraction Answer Key

*Note: Answers read across, per page.*

**58–59** 2, 1, 3; 1, 3, 4; 3, 3, 6; 2, 2, 4; 1, 4, 5; 4, 2, 6; 3, 4, 7; 1, 5, 6; 4, 3, 7

**60–61** 13, 15, 14, 12, 15, 16, 16, 17, 14, 15

**62–63** 12, 17, 13, 9, 13, 17, 9, 12

**64–65** 11, 11, 8, 9, 8, 10, 12, 9, 12, 10, 8, 11, 8, 9, 9, 12, 9, 11, 9, 12, 10, 10, 11;
a sea monster

**66–67** 16, 19, 17, 16, 15, 14, 19, 15, 11, 18, 18, 19, 16, 16, 13, 15, 14, 17, 14, 16, 17, 15, 16, 13, 18, 19, 17, 18, 17, 18, 12, 18

**68–69** 17, 19, 16, 14, 17, 15, 16, 12, 15, 11, 13, 17, 18, 18, 15, 14, 16, 13, 15, 19, 16, 19, 16, 17

**70–71** 12, 4, 16; 10, 3, 13; 14, 2, 16; 11, 6, 17; 15, 4, 19; 16, 1, 17; 12, 5, 17; 13, 6, 19; 12, 1, 13; 15, 3, 18; 16, 2, 18

**72–73** time to run, act like a banana, all of them, palm trees, thanks a bunch

**74–75** 3, 1, 2; 4, 2, 2; 5, 2, 3; 4, 3, 1; 6, 4, 2; 5, 1, 4; 3, 2, 1; 5, 3, 2; 6, 3, 3; 5, 4, 1; 6, 1, 5

**76–77** 8, 6, 2; 9, 4, 5; 13, 6 ,7; 10, 3, 7; 11, 3, 8; 11, 7, 4; 12, 6, 6; 10, 5, 5; 13, 5, 8

**78–79** 9, 6, 3, 7, 13, 8, 4, 0, 9, 8, 5, 10, 9, 11, 9, 15, 4, 5, 8, 7

**80–81** 5, 5, 7; 1, 1, 4; 2, 2, 6; 4, 4, 5; 4, 4, 8; 6, 6, 9

**82–83** −, −, +, −, −, +, −, +, +, −, −, +, +, +, −, −, +, +, −, −, +, +, +

**84–85** true, false, true, false, false, true, false, true, true, false, true, false

**86–87** See below.

**88–89** See below.

**90–91** 10, 4, 6; 13, 8, 5; 15, 6, 9; 11, 6, 5; 12, 7, 5; 10, 3, 7; 16, 8, 8; 14, 6, 8; 10, 6, 4; 17, 9, 8; 12, 6, 6; 15, 8, 7

**92–93** 19, 5, 16, 17, 18, 9, 14, 19, 5, 18, 7, 12, 9, 12, 7, 8

**94–95** See below.

**96–97** 1. 8, 2. 4, 3. 18, 4. 17, 5. 4, 6. 17

**98–99** Color: 9, 1, 8, 8, 13, 15, 4, 12, 11, 5, 18, 10, 19, 0, 2, 16

**100–101** 11, 7, 18, 12, 15, 12, 14, 13

**102–103** 12, 12, 9, 16, 5, 8, 17, 11, 14, 6, 5, 15, 14, 12, 9, 12, 8, 10, 21, 14

**104–105** 7, 5, 12; 10, 5, 15; 4, 5, 7, 16; 12, 5, 7; 16, 9, 7; 9, 9,18

**106–107** 20, 50, 50, 40, 70, 70, 70, 90, 40, 60, 60, 80, 70, 80, 90, 60, 80, 90, 80, 90

**108–109** 10, 20, 30, 10, 10, 40, 20, 50, 30, 30, 20, 40, 60, 10, 40

**110–111** 50, 10, 40, 30, 20, 80, 80, 40, 70, 70

**112–113** 5, 70, 10, 11, 30, 9, 80, 14, 90, 14, 15, 10, 15, 15, 14, 17, 70, 9, 30, 30, 18, 20, 20, 3, 10, 40, 6, 50, 50, 20, 6, 70

**86–87**

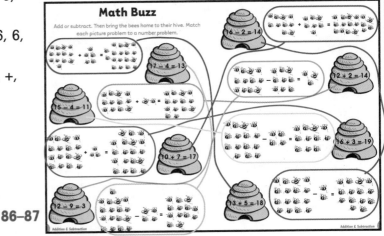

**88–89**

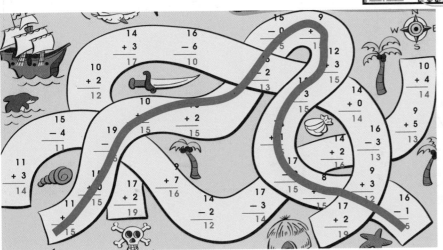

**94–95**

# Who's Who

Look at the picture of each animal pair. Read the question. Circle the correct animal.

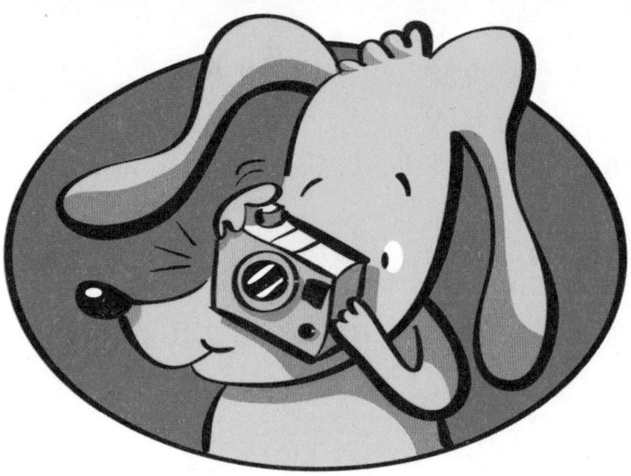

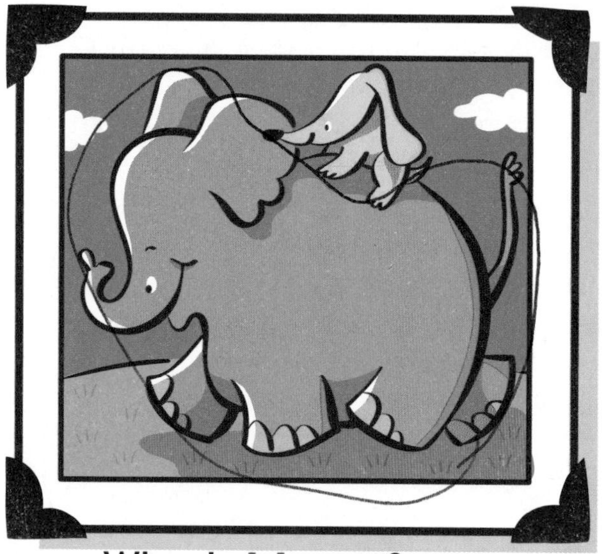

1 Who is **bigger**?

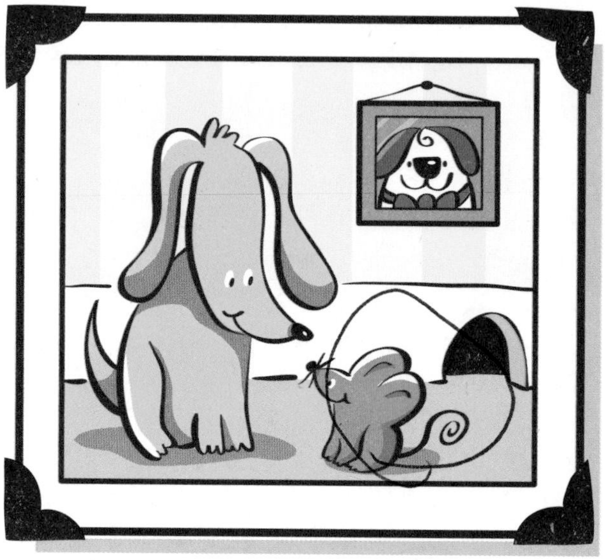

2 Who is **smaller**?

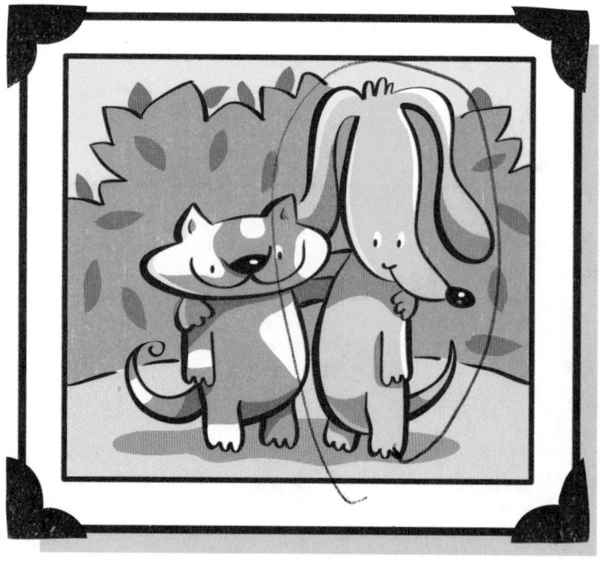

3 Who is **bigger**?

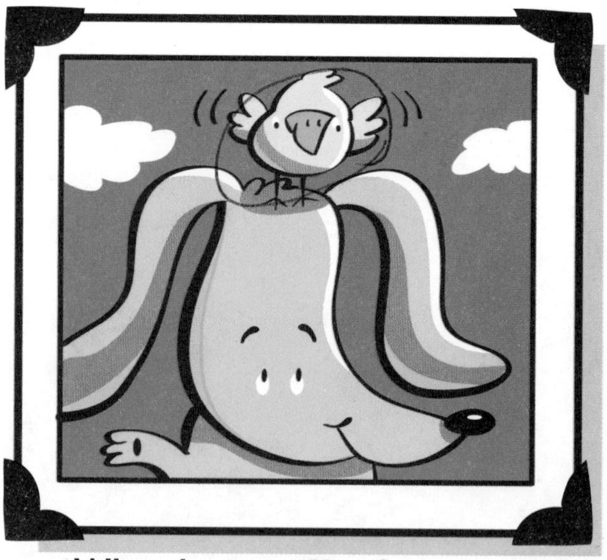

4 Who is **smaller**?

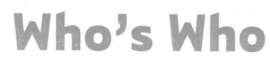

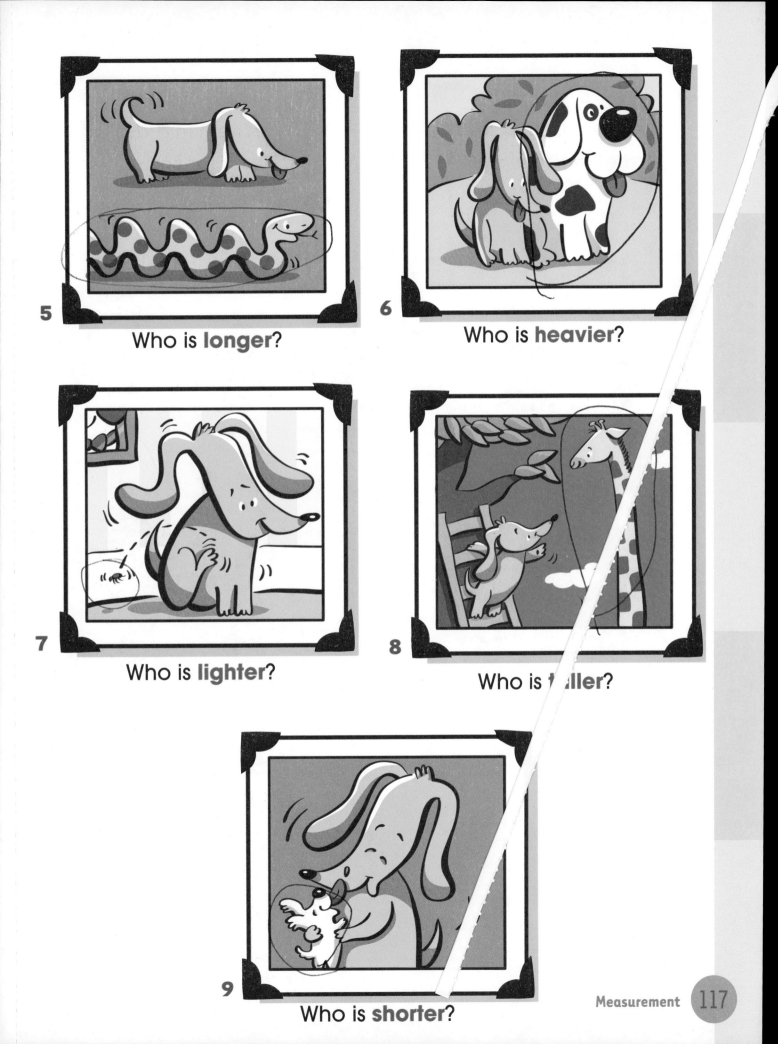

**5** Who is **longer**?

**6** Who is **heavier**?

**7** Who is **lighter**?

**8** Who is **taller**?

**9** Who is **shorter**?

# Size It Up

Look at each set of nesting dolls. Put them in order from **smallest** to **biggest**, using numbers. Use **1** for the smallest, up to **5** for the biggest.

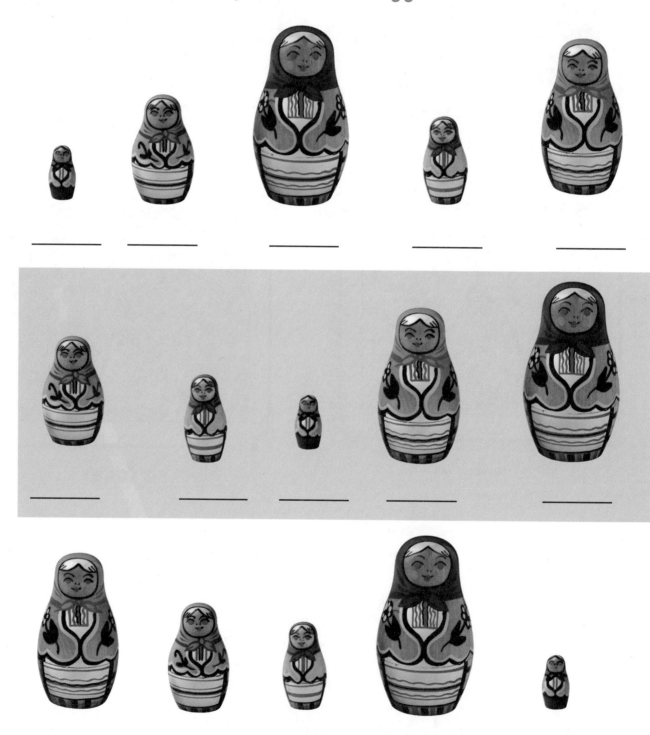

_____    _____    _____    _____    _____

_____    _____    _____    _____    _____

_____    _____    _____    _____

Now put each column of dolls in order from **biggest** to **smallest**, using numbers. Use **1** for the biggest, up to **5** for the smallest.

# Measure Match

Circle the better answer.
See page 121 if you need help.

I'd like to weigh my dog.

I'll use a

I want to make curtains.
How tall is this window?

I'll use a

What is today's date?

I'll use a

How cold is it outside?

I'll use a

I need to measure milk for a cake.

I'll use a

How long is this candy bar?

I'll use a

# Measuring Tools

## Measuring Cup and Spoons

Use these to measure foods when you cook.

## Ruler

Use this to measure things shorter than your hand.

## Measuring Tape

Use this to measure things longer than your hand.

## Scale

Use this to weigh things.

## Calendar

Use this to count days, weeks, months, and years.

## Thermometer

Use this to measure hot and cold.

# Lizard Lengths

Look at each column of lizards. Put them in size order.
Write **short**, **longer**, or **longest** under each one.

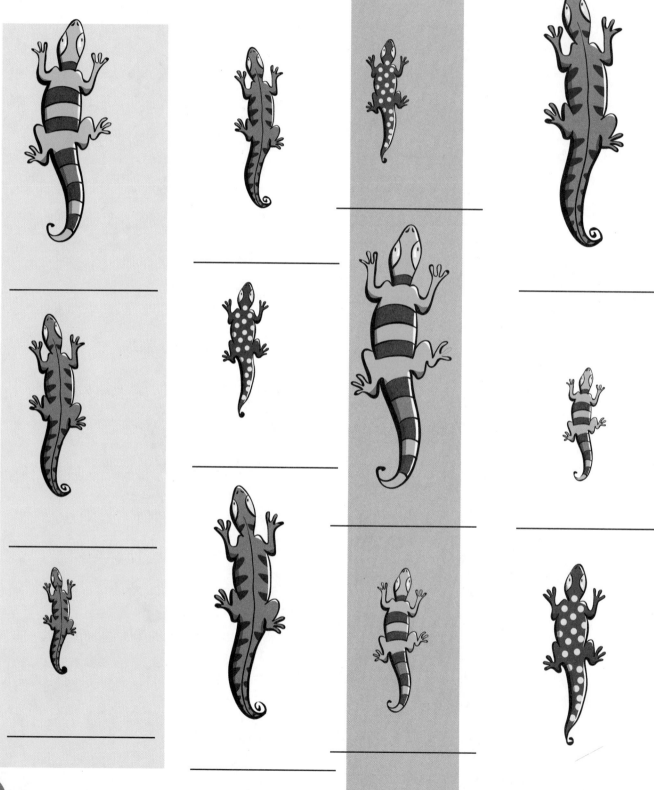

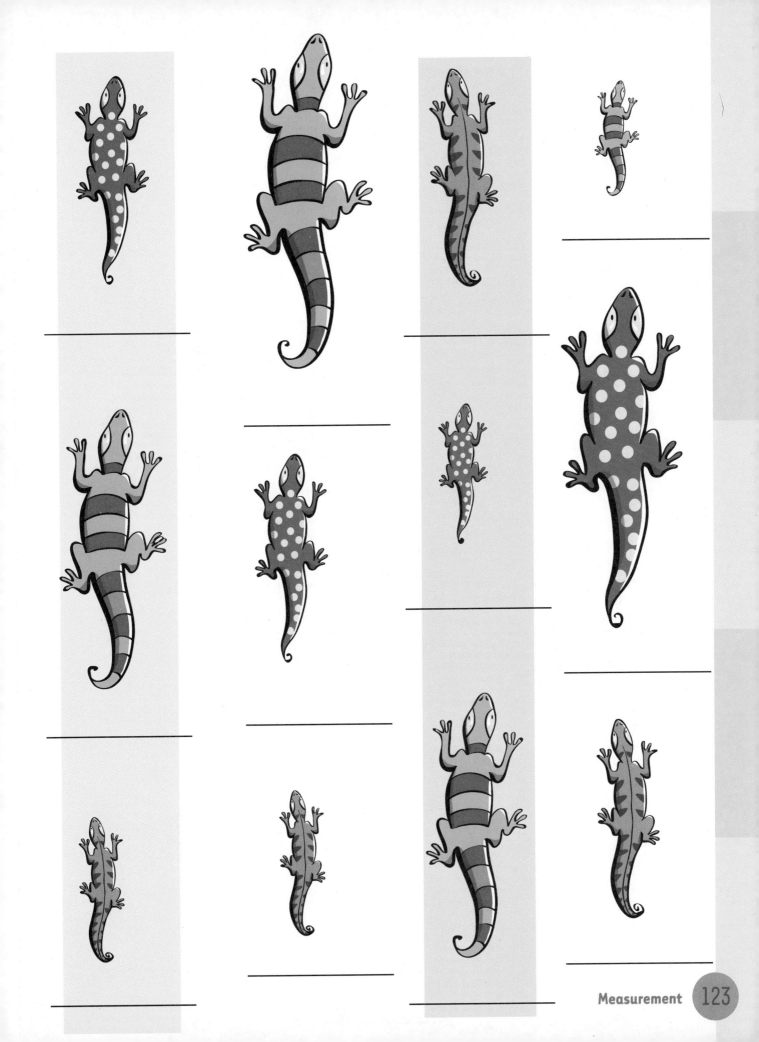

# More or Less?

Look at each pair. Which one has more inside?
Write **more** or **less** under each picture.

_____    _____

_____    _____

_____    _____

_____    _____

_____ _____

_____ _____

_____ _____

_____ _____

# Larger or Smaller?

Look at the pictures. Which one is larger?
Write **larger** or **smaller** under each picture.

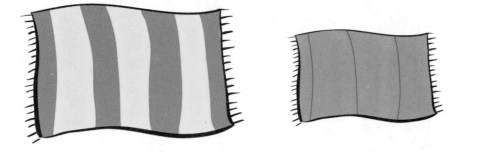

_____        _____

_____        _____

_____        _____

_____        _____

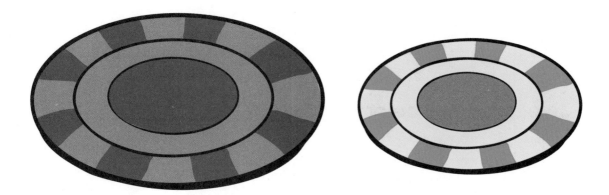

_____        _____

        _____

_____

# Week Speak

1. How many days are in one week? _____

2. Which is the first day of the week? _____

3. Which is the last day of the week? _____

4. Which day comes after Wednesday? _____

5. Which comes first, Tuesday or Thursday? _____

6. Which day comes before Saturday? _____

These kids are showing the days of the week.
Look at the days. Answer the questions.

7. Which day usually starts the school week? _____

8. Which day comes after Tuesday? _____

9. What day comes after Wednesday and before Friday?

_____

10. What is your favorite day of the week? _____

Why? _____

_____

_____

# One Busy Kid!

| Sunday | Monday | Tuesday | Wednesday |
|---|---|---|---|
| 1 | 2 Science Museum Field Trip | 3 | 4 |
| 8 | 9 | 10 | 11 |
| 15 | 16 Mom's Birthday! | 17 | 18 |
| 22 | 23 | 24 | 25 |
| 29 | 30 No School! | 31 | |

1. How many days are in this month? _____

2. On which day of the week does Maya have piano lessons?

   _____

3. What will Maya do on Friday the 13th? _____

130 Measurement

# Read Maya's calendar. Answer the questions.

| Thursday | Friday | Saturday |
|---|---|---|
| 5 Art Class | 6 | 7 Scout Meeting |
| 12 Scout Bake Sale | 13 Visit Grandma and Grandpa | 14 |
| 19 Skate Park | 20 | 21 |
| 26 | 27 | 28 Sleep-over Party |

4. Which comes first: Maya's scout meeting, or the sleep-over

   party? _____

5. On what date will Maya go to the skate park?

   _____

6. Maya wants to join the soccer team. She must practice on
   the same day every week. Write the words "soccer team" on
   the days you think Maya should practice.

# You're Getting Warmer

A thermometer measures temperature in degrees. Read the degrees next to each picture. Write **cold**, **warm**, or **hot** for each temperature.

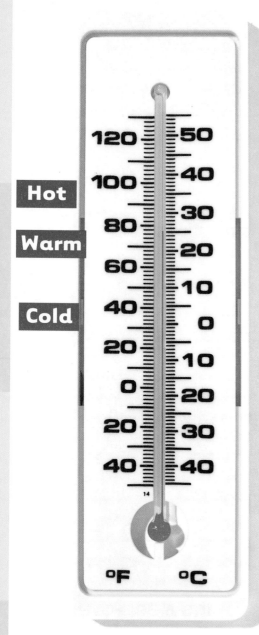

Hot

Warm

Cold

°F    °C

90 degrees _____

30 degrees _____

100 degrees

_____

70 degrees

_____

60 degrees

_____

65 degrees

_____

0 degrees _____

# You Rule!

An **inch** is a standard unit of length. We measure inches with a ruler. Measure each item. Write how long it is in inches.

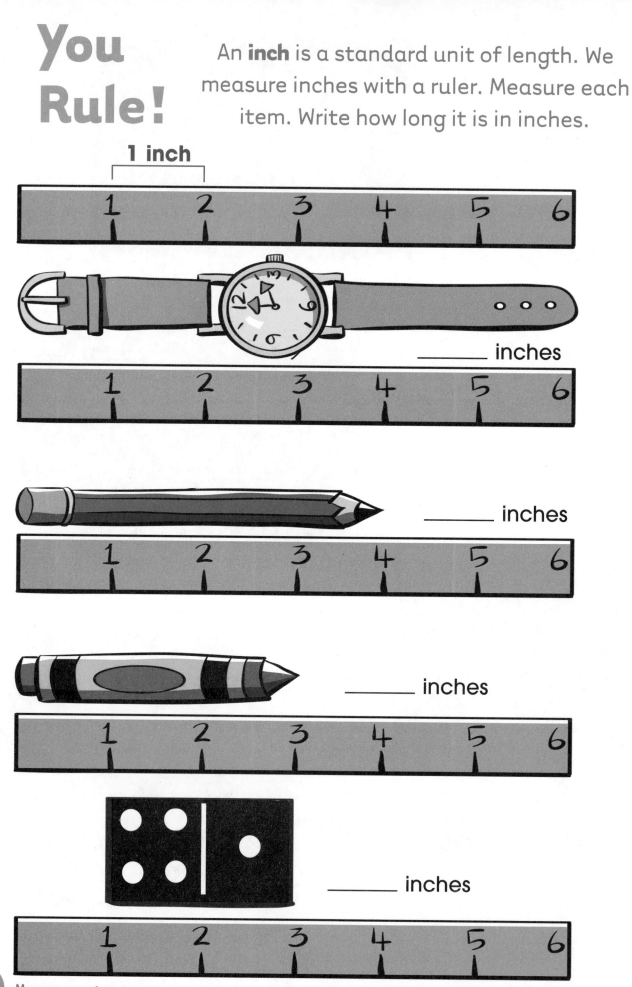

1 inch

1  2  3  4  5  6

_____ inches

1  2  3  4  5  6

_____ inches

1  2  3  4  5  6

_____ inches

1  2  3  4  5  6

_____ inches

1  2  3  4  5  6

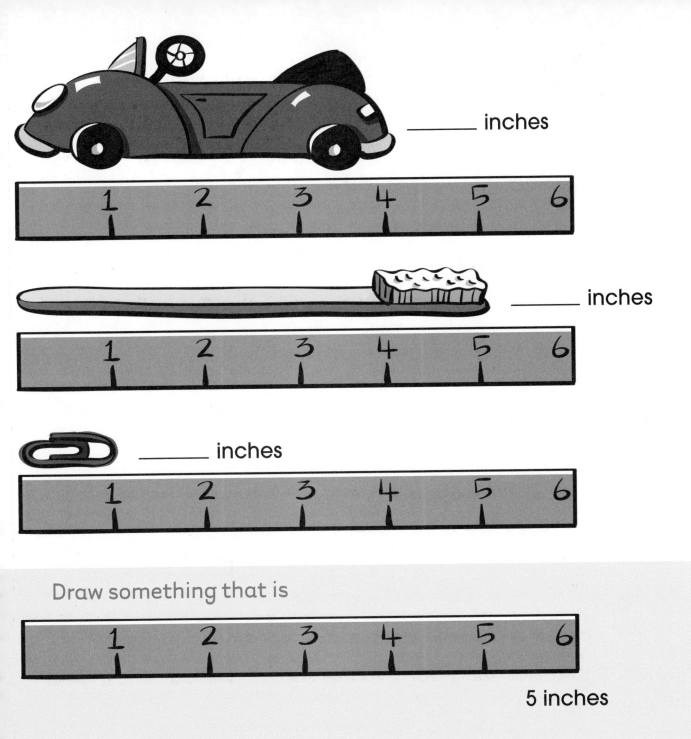

_____ inches

_____ inches

_____ inches

Draw something that is

5 inches

# The Rainy Day

Read the story. When you see **bold** words, (circle) the answer that makes sense.

"Look outside," said my friend Sam. "It is raining. It's cold, too. That **measuring cup thermometer** shows that it's just 40 **degrees inches**!

"I know," I said. "It's boring when it rains. There is nothing to do. We are stuck inside."

"Who's bored?" asked my mom. She came into the room. "I have an idea," my mother said. "Why don't you two make a castle?"

"A castle?" asked Sam.

"How do we do that?" I added.

"Start with a blanket and a table," said Mom. "You'll figure out the rest."

We grabbed a blanket. We threw it over the dining room table. The blanket hung down to the floor on all four sides. We crawled inside.

"Here we are in our castle," I said. "We just need to fix it up!"

"How?" Sam asked.

"Measure that piece of cardboard with a **tape measure scale**," I told him. "Then we'll make some **cold big** towers with it."

Sam measured the cardboard and cut it out. I made one tower, but it was too **small hot**. I made another tower that was a bit **warmer larger**. It looked great.

Sam got to work, too. He measured pieces on ten sheets of colored paper with a **thermometer ruler**. He cut out the pieces. He taped the pieces to a **long tall** piece of string.

"Look!" said Sam. "I made some flags for the castle. Do you like them?"

"Yes, I do!" I said. I tried to hang the flags above the castle, but I was too **big short** to reach. I climbed on a chair. Then I was **tall warm** enough to hang the flags.

Suddenly, I had a great idea. I ran to the kitchen. I took five bowls from the shelf. I put the bowls in a circle around our castle. Then I filled a **calendar measuring cup** with water. I used it to fill the bowls.

"Wow, what is that?" asked Sam.

"It's our moat!" I said.

Mom came in. "Wow!" she said. "You two sure know how to build a castle."

"We sure do!" I said. "I hope it rains tomorrow, too!"

# The Big Parade

Everyone loves a parade.
Cut out the cards. Put them in a line from the
shortest clown or creature to the tallest.

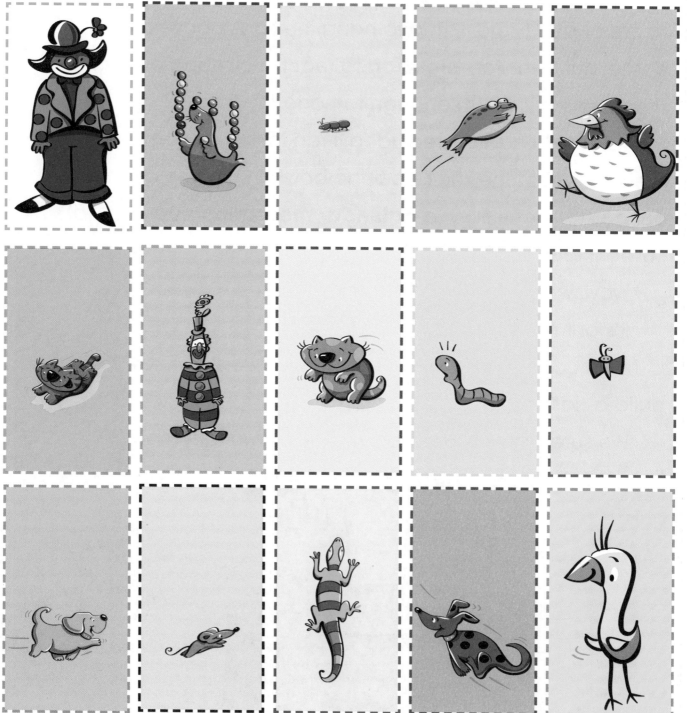

Think of some other ways you could
order the parade. Try them.

# Measurement Answer Key

**116–117 Circle** 1. elephant, 2. mouse, 3. dog, 4. bird, 5. snake, 6. bigger dog, right, 7. flea, 8. giraffe, 9. puppy, left

**118–119** 1, 3, 5, 2, 4; 3, 2, 1, 4, 5; 4, 3, 2, 5, 1; 2, 1, 5, 4, 3; 4, 2, 1, 3, 5; 3, 5, 2, 4, 1

**120–121 Circle** scale, measuring tape, calendar, thermometer, measuring cup, ruler

**122–123** longest, longer, short; longer, short, longest; short, longest, longer; longest, short, longer; longer, longest, short; longest, longer, short; longer, short, longest; short, longest, longer

**124–125** less, more; less, more; more, less; less, more; less, more; more, less; more, less; less, more

**126–127** larger, smaller; smaller, larger; larger, smaller; larger, smaller; larger, smaller; smaller, larger

**128–129** 1. 7, 2. Sunday, 3. Saturday, 4. Thursday, 5. Tuesday, 6. Friday, 7. Monday, 8. Wednesday, 9. Thursday; 10. answers will vary.

**130–131** 1. 31, 2. Tuesday, 3. visit Grandma and Grandpa; 4. the scout meeting; 5. 19, 6. soccer team could appear every Monday, Wednesday, Friday, or Sunday

**132–133** cold, hot, hot, warm, warm, warm, cold

**134–135** 6, 4, 3, 2, 4, 5, 1; drawings will vary.

**136–137 Circle** thermometer, degrees, tape measure, big, small, larger, ruler, long, short, tall, measuring cup

# All Around Town

Look at the picture. Circle the correct answer.

What's **above** the buildings?   plane   bird   dog

Who's **outside** the house?   man   plant   cat

Who's **inside** the house?   man   plant   cat

What's **on** the car?   cat   bird   dog

What's **under** the cat?   car   cupcake   crate

Which dog is **near** the cat?   dog on the left   dog on the right

Which dog is **far** from the cat?   dog on the left   dog on the right

What's **below** the big sign?   bread   plane   cat

# Shape Up

Which shapes are the same?
Draw a line between them.

# Different Dinos

(Circle) 5 dinosaurs that don't match the others.

# Blast Off!

A **triangle** has three sides.

Follow the triangles through the maze.
Get the rocket from **Start** to **Finish**.

# Get into Shape

A **circle** is a round shape.

Draw some circles here.

A **square** has four sides.
All of the sides are the same size.

Draw some squares here.

A **triangle** has three sides.

Draw some triangles here.

A **rectangle** has four sides.

Draw some rectangles here.

# A Square Meal

Can you find the shapes on this tray?

Draw a ◯ around each **circle**.

Draw a △ around each **triangle**.

Draw a ▭ around each **rectangle**.

Draw a ◻ around each **square**.

# Pattern Power

Draw the next shapes in each pattern.

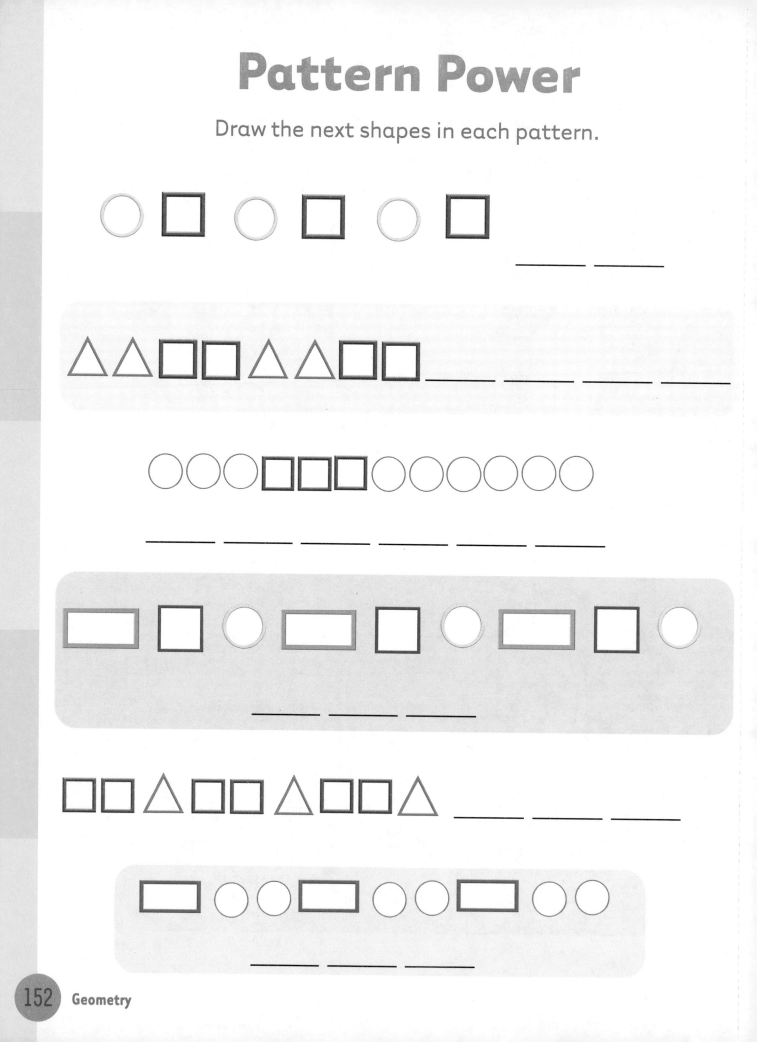

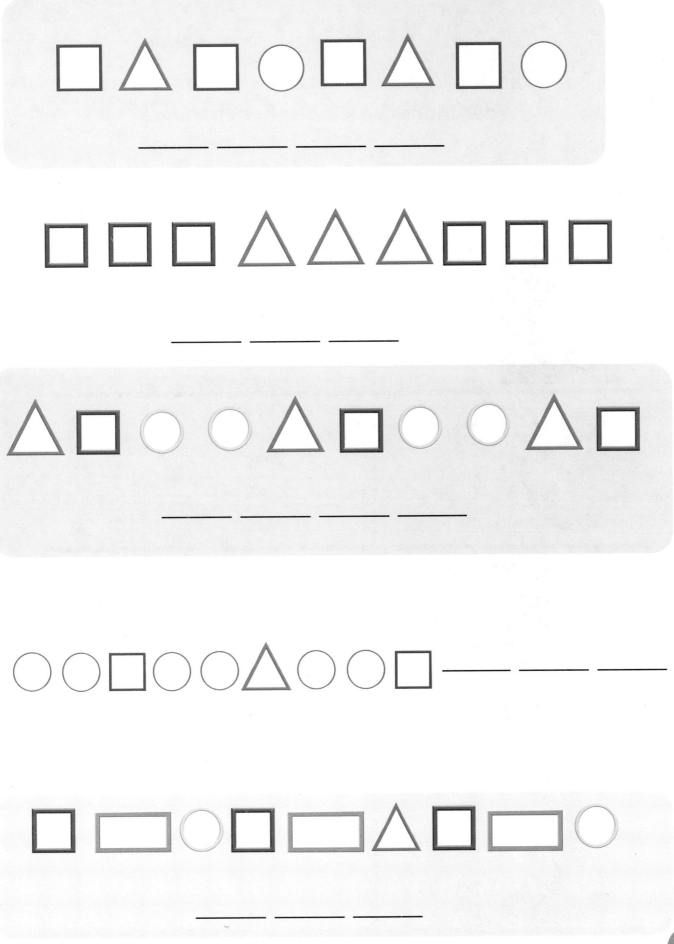

# You Name It

Put a check ✓ in the column under the word that best describes the shape of each thing.

| | ◯ Circle | △ Triangle | ▭ Rectangle | ⬜ Square |
|---|---|---|---|---|
| (checkerboard) | | | | |
| (beach ball) | | | | |
| (quilt) | | | | |
| (teepee) | | | | |

| | Circle | Triangle | Rectangle | Square |
|---|---|---|---|---|
|  | | | | |
|  | | | | |
|  | | | | |
|  | | | | |
|  | | | | |

# Water Colors

Color each thing with a

◯ yellow ▢ purple

△ red ▭ blue.

# That Looks Like . . .

Draw lines to match each picture to a solid shape in the box.

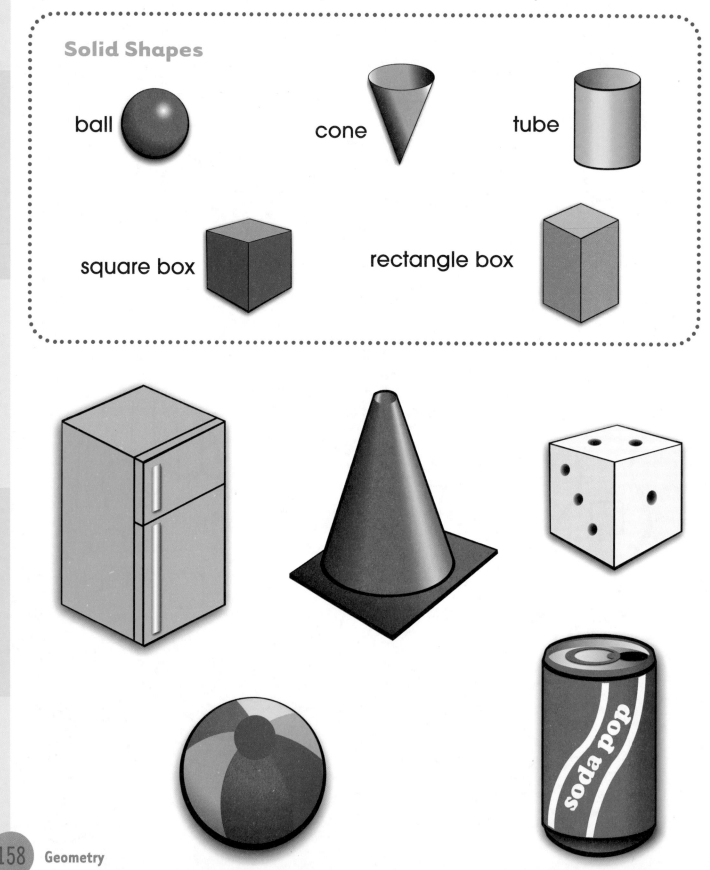

**Solid Shapes**

ball

cone

tube

square box

rectangle box

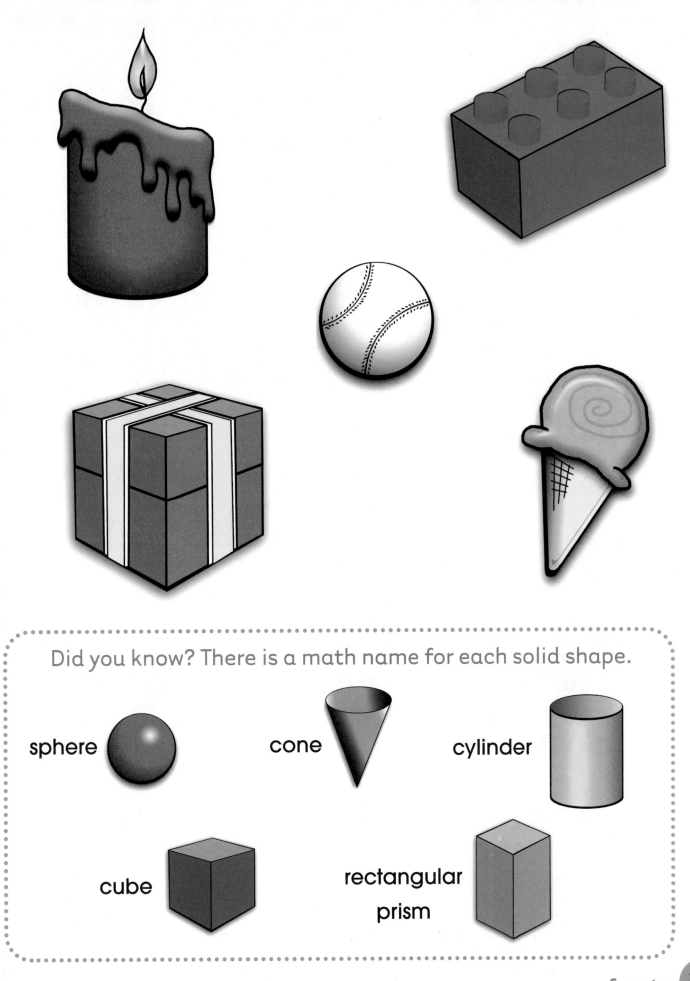

Did you know? There is a math name for each solid shape.

sphere

cone

cylinder

cube

rectangular
prism

# Try a Tangram!

Cut out the tangram shapes.
Can you use the shapes
to make these pictures?

What other pictures can you make?

# Geometry Answer Key

**140–141** **Circle:** plane; cat, man, bird, crate; dog on the left; dog on the right, bread
**142–143** **See below.**
**144–145** **See below.**
**146–147** **See below.**
**146–147** **See below.**
**148–149** Drawings will vary.
**150–151** Draw as indicated; **see below.**
**152–153** **See below.**
**154–155** **Check:** rectangle or square, circle, rectangle, triangle, circle, rectangle or square, triangle, square, rectangle
**156–157** Coloring reveals fish in aquarium; fish
**158–159** **See below.**

**142–143**

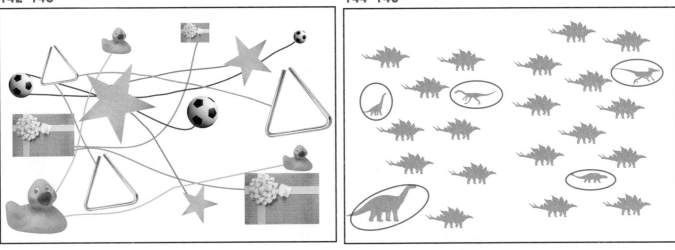

**144–145**

**146–147**

**150–151**

**152–153**

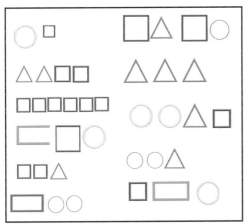

**158–159**

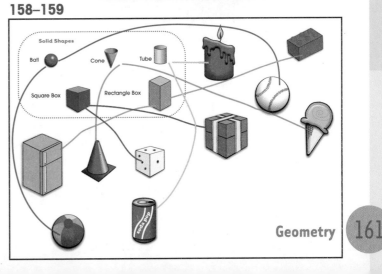

# Bank On It!

Write the name of each coin.
Tell how much it's worth.

penny    1 cent    1¢

nickel    5 cents    5¢

dime    10 cents    10¢

quarter    25 cents    25¢

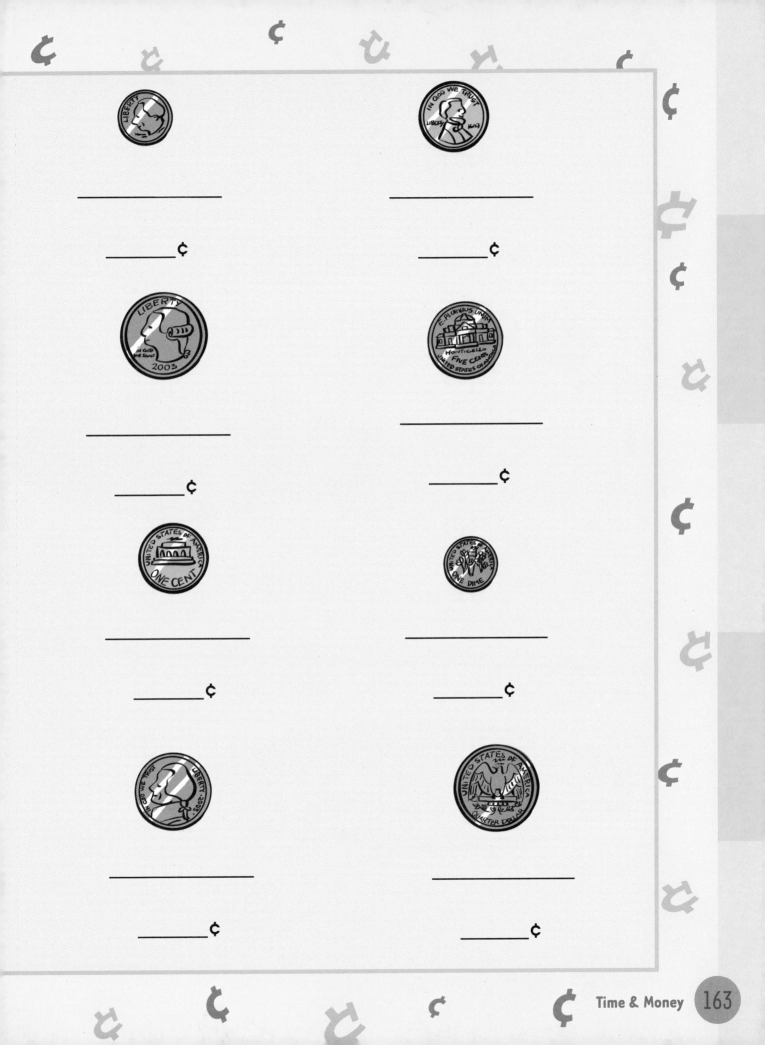

# How Much Is Here?

Add up the coins. Write the amount.
Don't forget the ¢ sign!

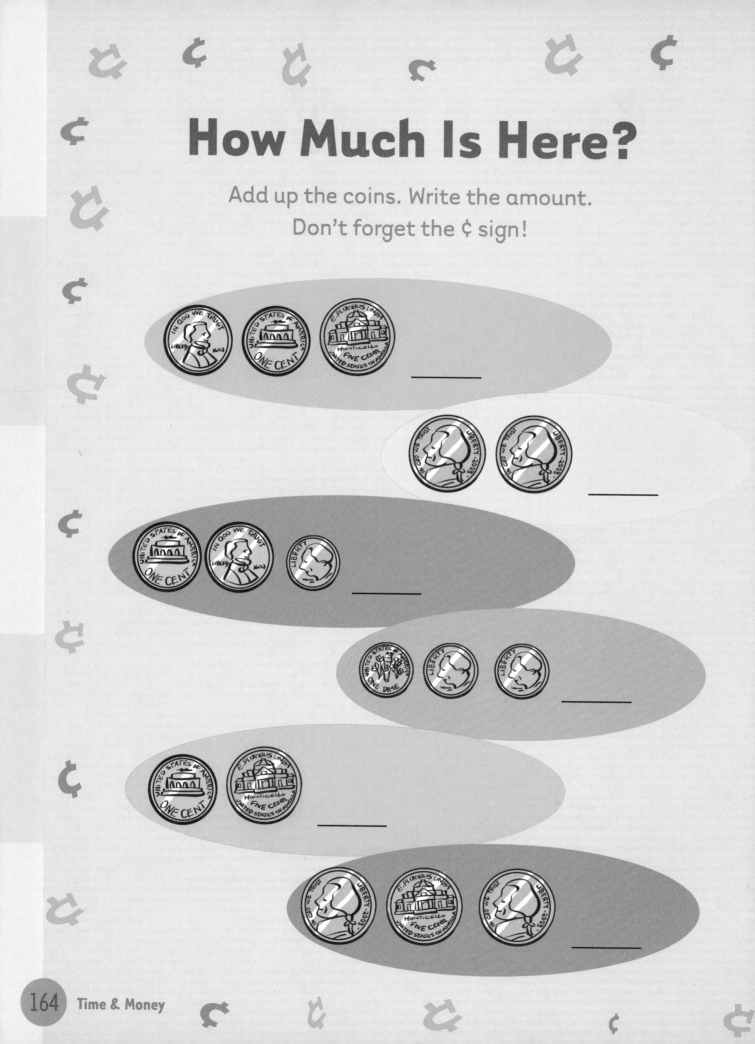

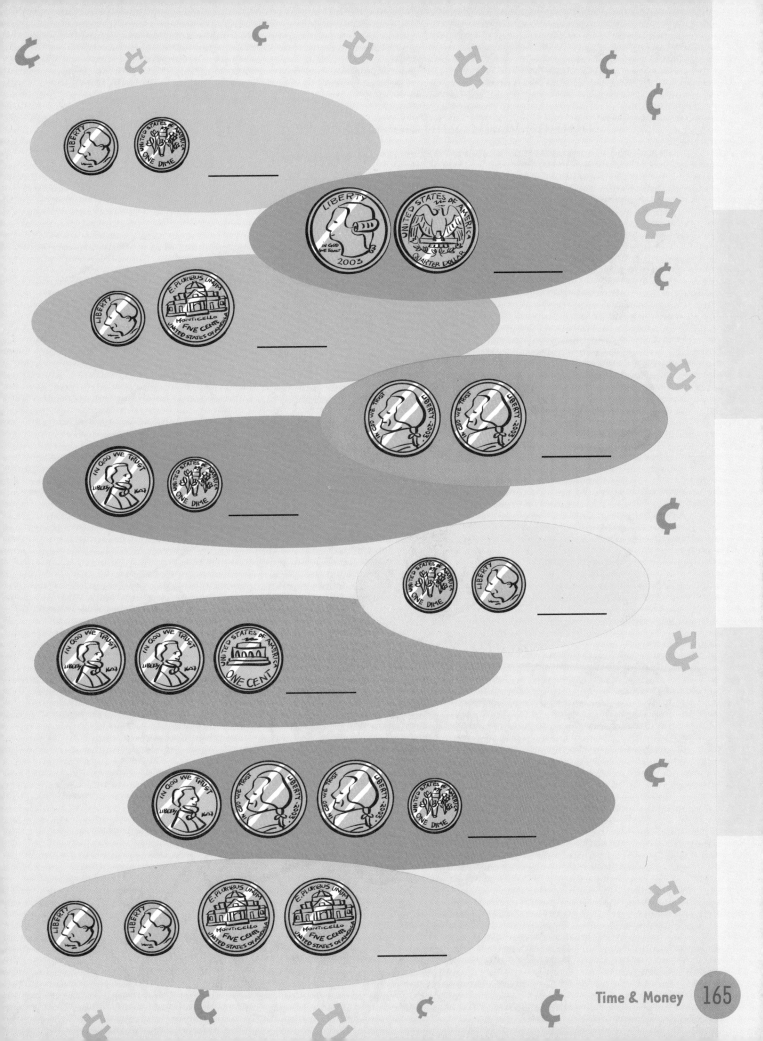

# A Really, Really Big Sale!

Imagine you could buy these things just with coins!
Add up the coins. Write the price on each tag.

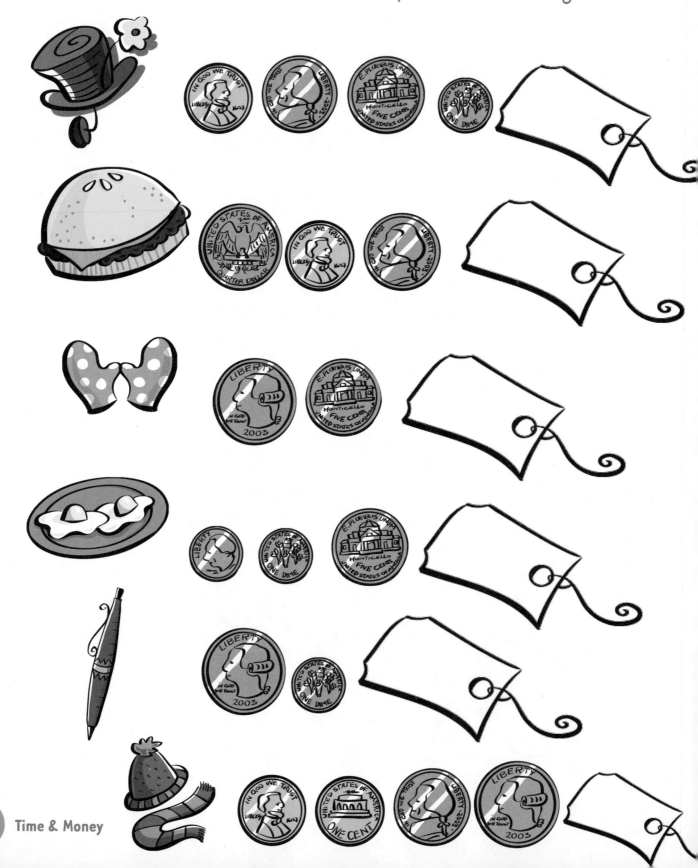

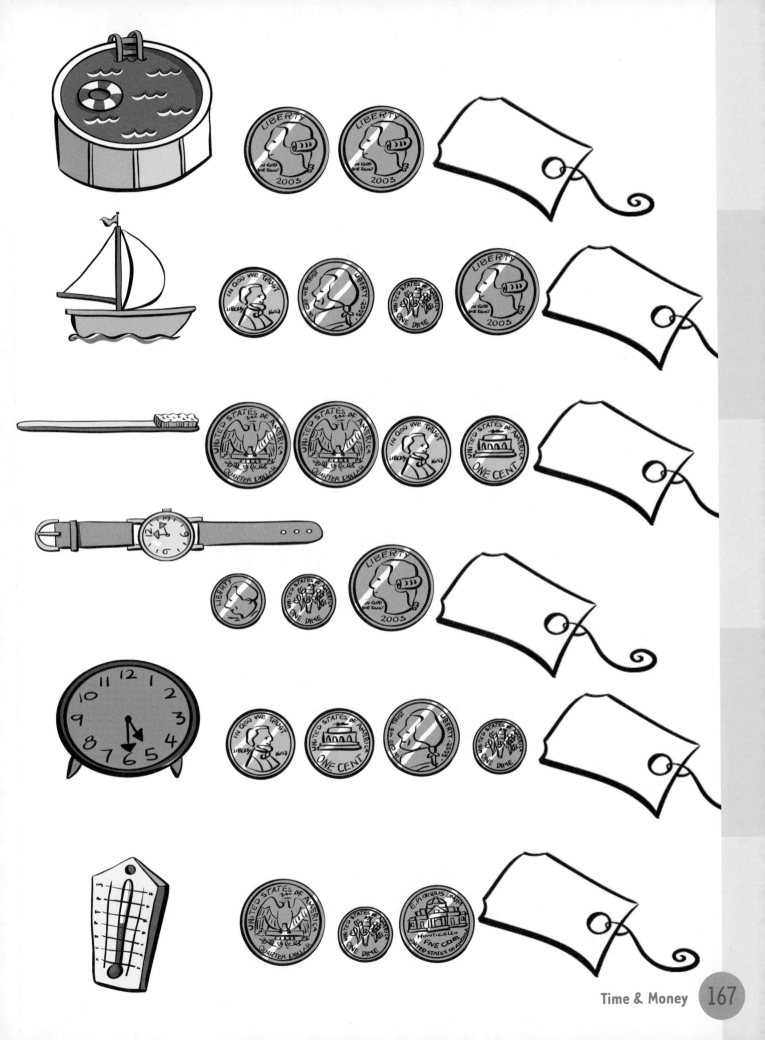

# Snack Time

(Circle) the coins you need to buy each snack.

52¢

60¢

50¢

75¢

85¢

37¢

48¢

63¢

71¢

55¢

# Silly Stamps

Draw a line from each stamp to its value.

thirty-two cents

fifty-five cents

twenty-five cents

fifteen cents

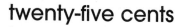

ninety cents

one cent

nineteen cents

seventy-one cents

forty-four cents

twenty cents

sixty-three cents

# Money Monkey Business

Is the problem true or false? <u>Underline</u> the monkey that has the correct answer.

= 52¢

true    false

= 13¢

true    false

= 99¢

true    false

= 23¢

true    false

= 87¢

true    false

= 45¢

true    false

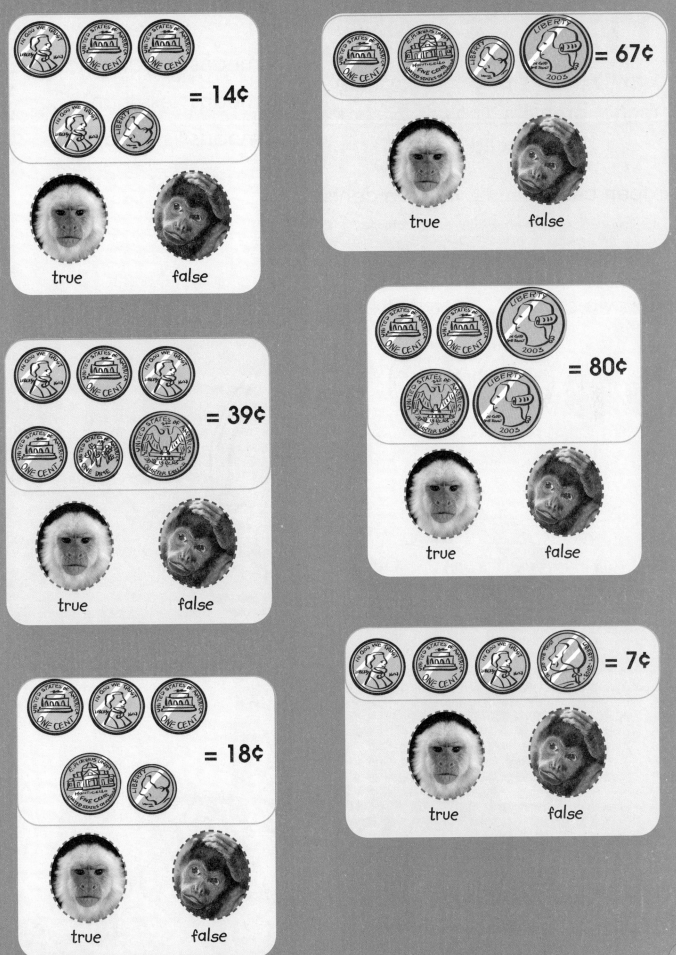

= 14¢

true    false

= 67¢

true    false

= 39¢

true    false

= 80¢

true    false

= 18¢

true    false

= 7¢

true    false

# Pirate's Gold

Draw **>**, **<**, or **=** to complete each money problem. Look at the box if you need help.

> **>** means "greater than"
>
> **<** means "less than"
>
> **=** means "is equal to"

sixteen cents _____ thirteen cents

87¢ _____ 90¢

thirty-two cents _____ twenty-three cents

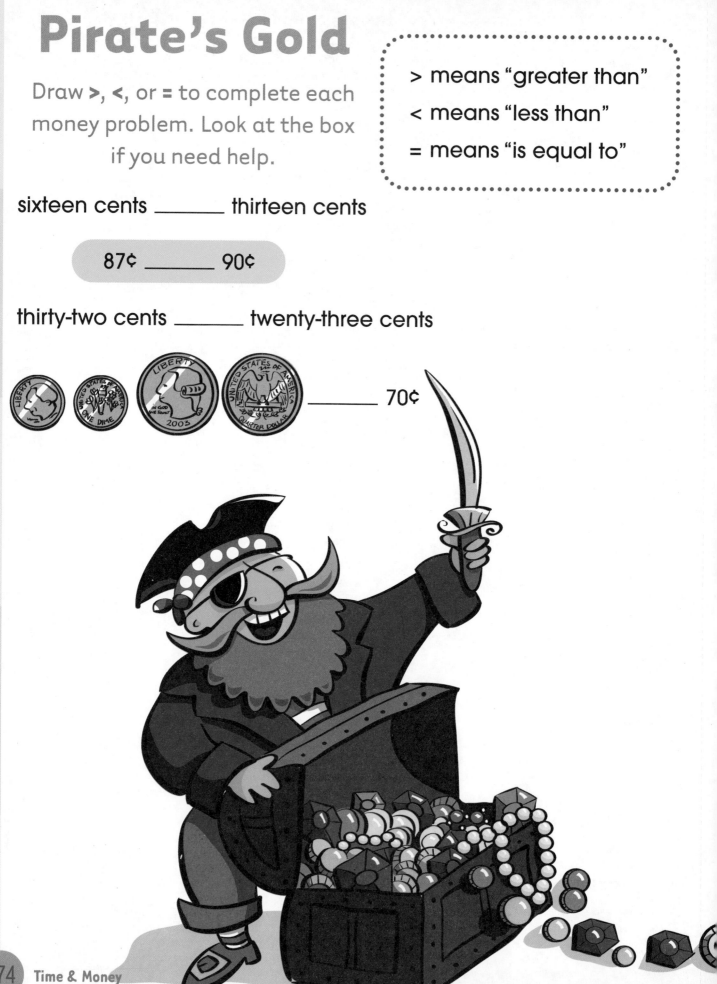

_____ 70¢

thirty-two cents _____ twenty-three cents

45¢ _____ 48¢

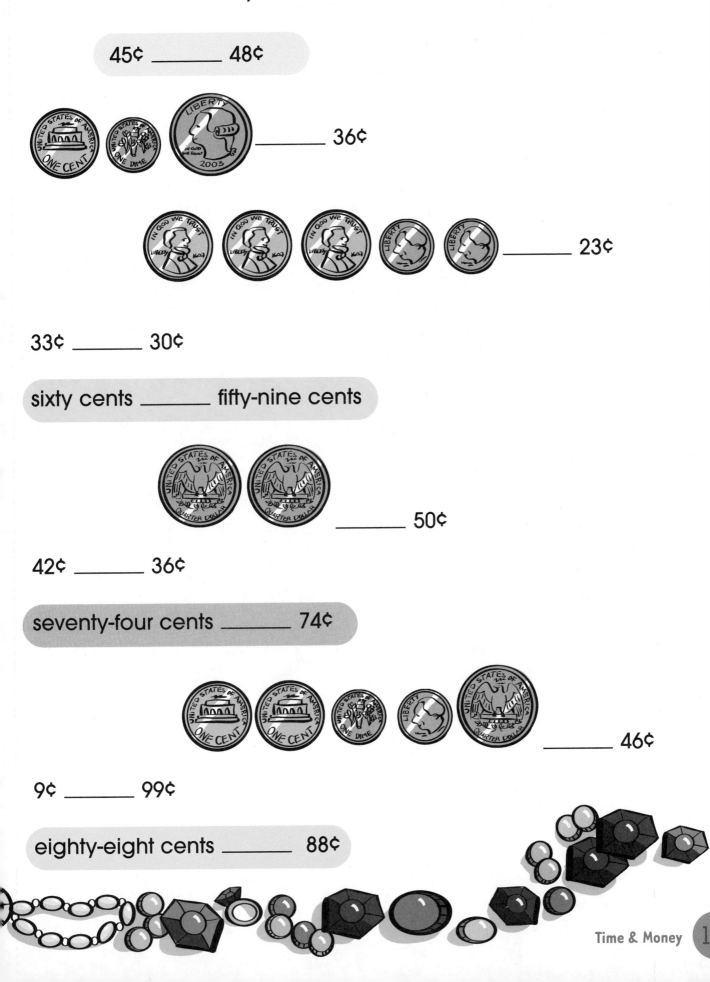

_____ 36¢

_____ 23¢

33¢ _____ 30¢

sixty cents _____ fifty-nine cents

_____ 50¢

42¢ _____ 36¢

seventy-four cents _____ 74¢

_____ 46¢

9¢ _____ 99¢

eighty-eight cents _____ 88¢

# Coin Crisscross

Write the money amounts in numbers in the grid.
The Across numbers go left to right.
The Down numbers go up and down.

## ACROSS

1. eighty-four cents
3. nineteen cents
5. thirty-five cents
7. two cents
8. seven cents
9. fifty-one cents
10. six cents
11. four cents
12. ninety-seven cents
14. five cents
15. eight cents
16. three cents

## DOWN

2. forty-five cents
3. fifteen cents
4. nine cents
5. thirty-seven cents
6. thirty-one cents
7. twenty-three cents
9. fifty-four cents
10. sixty-four cents
12. ninety-three cents
13. one cent

# Day or Night?

Tell whether each picture shows **day** or **night**. Write the word on the line.

Do homework _____

Get dressed

_____

Look at the moon _____

Come home from school _____

Put on pajamas _____

Go to sleep _____

Go to sports practice

_____

Eat breakfast

_____

The sun comes up _____

Eat lunch _____

Go to school _____

Eat dinner _____

How many of the things you wrote **day** next to happen in the morning?

_____

# Tick-Tock Shop

Any time is a good time at the Tick-Tock Shop. Write the time below each clock. Write the time in two ways.

When the big hand of a clock points to 12, the small hand tells the hour. This clock is showing **4 o'clock**, or **4:00**.

_____ o'clock

_____:_____

_____ o'clock

_____:_____

_____ o'clock

_____:_____

_____ o'clock

_____:_____

_____ o'clock

_____:_____

_____ o'clock

_____:_____

_____ o'clock

_____:_____

_____ o'clock

_____:_____

_____ o'clock

_____:_____

# Time for Me to . . .

Write the time, ending in **o'clock**, next to each clock.

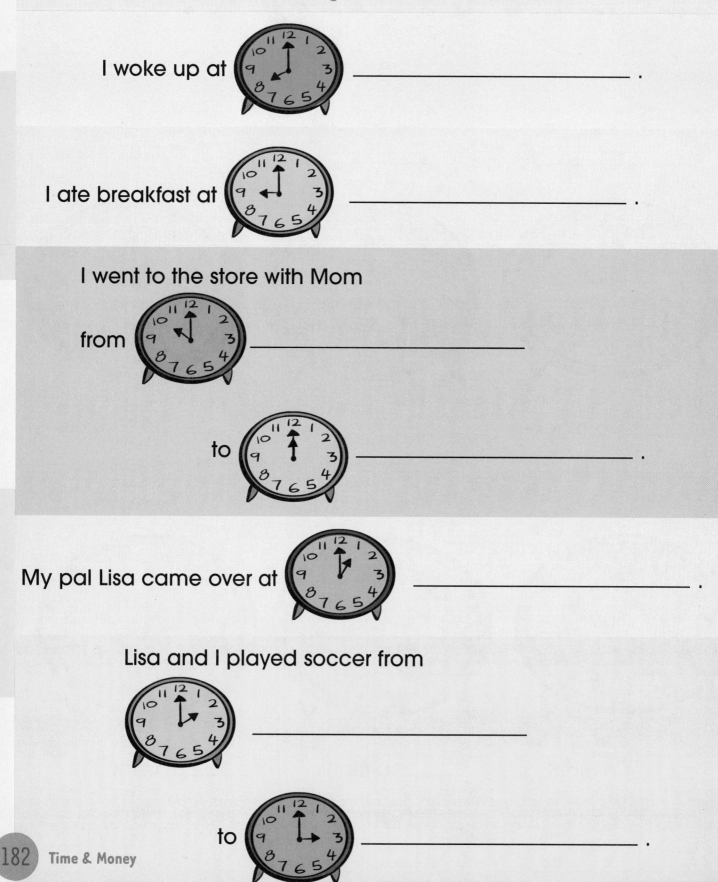

I woke up at _____ .

I ate breakfast at _____ .

I went to the store with Mom

from _____

to _____ .

My pal Lisa came over at _____ .

Lisa and I played soccer from

_____

to _____ .

Lisa left at  _____ .

I cleaned my room at  _____ .

My family and I ate dinner at  _____ .

We all watched TV from  _____

to  _____ .

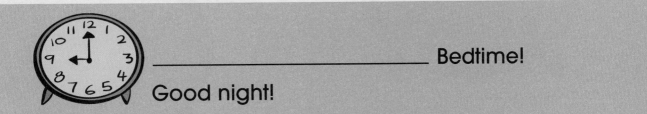 _____ Bedtime!

Good night!

# On the Hour

Draw the hands on each clock. Remember: The big hand will point to 12. The small hand will point to the hour.

3 o'clock

10 o'clock

1 o'clock

2 o'clock

8 o'clock

4 o'clock

6 o'clock

11 o'clock

12 o'clock

5 o'clock

7 o'clock

9 o'clock

Draw a clock with your favorite time.
Tell why you like that hour.

_____

_____

_____

# In Half the Time

Write the time below each clock.
Write the time in two ways.

When the big hand of a clock points to 6, the small hand tells the half hour. This clock is showing **seven-thirty,** or **7:30**.

_____-thirty

_____:_____

_____-thirty

_____:_____

_____-thirty

_____:_____

_____-thirty

_____:_____

_____-thirty

_____:_____

_____-thirty

_____:_____

_____-thirty

_____:_____

_____-thirty

_____:_____

_____-thirty

_____:_____

_____-thirty

_____:_____

_____-thirty

_____:_____

# Time for Some Fun

Draw a line from each clock to the correct half-hour time.

nine-thirty

one-thirty

three-thirty

four-thirty

 five-thirty

ten-thirty

seven-thirty

eight-thirty

twelve-thirty

 six-thirty

# Had a Great Time!

I spent the day at a theme park. Look at the clocks.
Read about what I did. Put each set in order.
Write **first**, **middle**, or **last** on the lines.

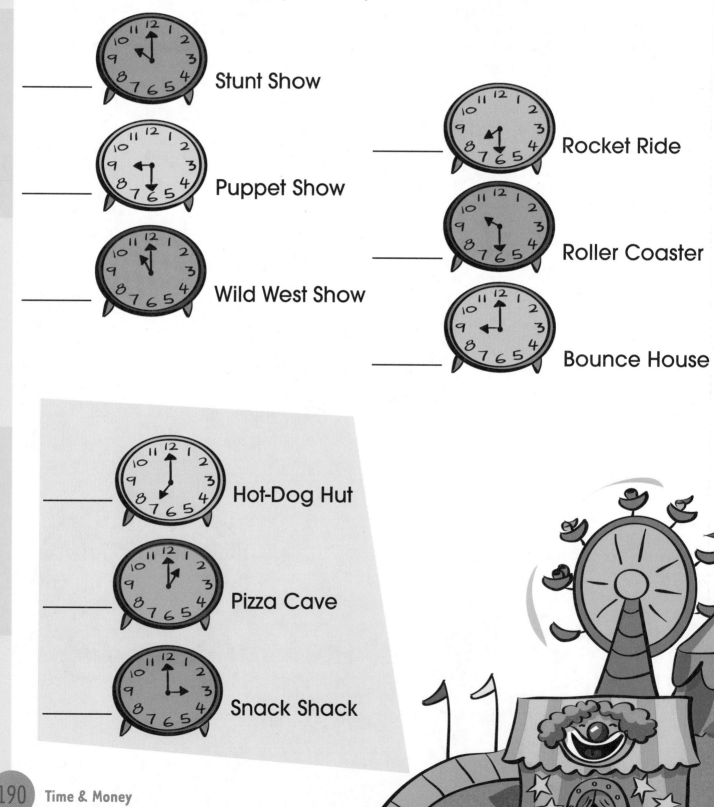

_____ Stunt Show

_____ Puppet Show

_____ Wild West Show

_____ Rocket Ride

_____ Roller Coaster

_____ Bounce House

_____ Hot-Dog Hut

_____ Pizza Cave

_____ Snack Shack

_____ 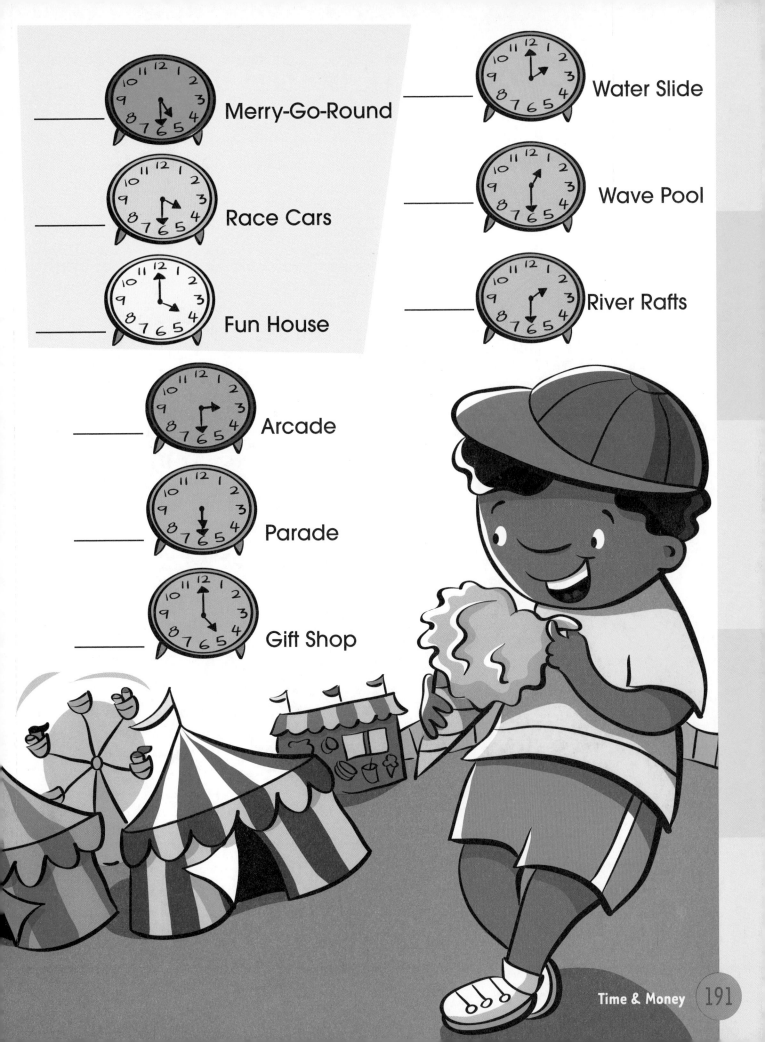 Merry-Go-Round

_____ Race Cars

_____ Fun House

_____ Water Slide

_____ Wave Pool

_____ River Rafts

_____ Arcade

_____ Parade

_____ Gift Shop

# Turtle Time

Read the time below each turtle.
Draw the hands on the turtle's shell to show that time.

10:30

4:00

1:00

11:30

2:00

# The Big Money Mix-Up

Read the story. Answer the questions.

Ella got some money for her birthday. "I'd like to buy a toy at the store," she said.

"I want to go, too." said her brother Adam.

The two children walked to the toy store.

Ella spent  on a purple pen at the store.

How much did the pen cost? _____

Ella also bought some trading cards for Adam.

She used ⬤⬤⬤⬤ to pay for the cards.

How much were the trading cards? _____

Adam looked at the games in the store.

He saw ⬤⬤⬤⬤ on the floor. He picked it up.

How much money did Adam find? _____

Outside, Ella saw something shiny. She saw

⬤⬤⬤⬤⬤⬤⬤⬤⬤ on the street.

She picked it up. How much money did Ella find? _____

Just then, Ella and Adam saw Sam. Sam looked sad.

"What's wrong, Sam?" asked Ella and Adam.

"I have a hole in my pocket," said Sam. "I lost some money."

The kids heard a man's voice. "I lost some money, too." It was Mr. Lane.

"Adam and I just found some money!" said Ella. "I wonder if it's yours. How much did you both lose?"

"I lost thirty-five cents," said Sam.

"I lost thirty-five cents, too," said Mr. Lane.

"We each found that much," said Ella. "Can you tell us more?"

Sam and Mr. Lane thought. Then Sam spoke. "I remember! I only had four coins."

"I had nine coins," said Mr. Lane.

"We know who has your money!" said Ella and Adam. "Here it is!"

"Thanks!" said Sam and Mr. Lane. "This was our lucky day."

Who found Sam's money? _____

Who found Mr. Lane's money? _____

# Three-Coin Challenge

Collect some nickels, dimes, and quarters. Use any 3 coins. Take turns answering the questions below. See how many answers you can find to the same question.

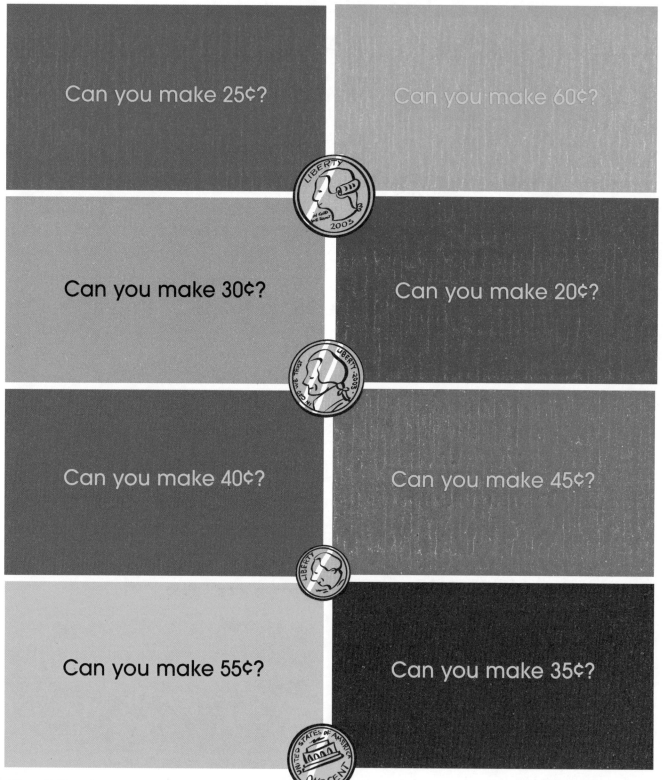

Can you make 25¢?

Can you make 60¢?

Can you make 30¢?

Can you make 20¢?

Can you make 40¢?

Can you make 45¢?

Can you make 55¢?

Can you make 35¢?

# Time & Money Answer Key

**162–163** dime, 10; penny, 1; quarter, 25; nickel, 5; penny, 1; dime, 10; nickel, 5; quarter, 25

**164–165** 7¢, 10¢, 12¢, 30¢, 6¢, 15¢, 20¢, 50¢, 15¢, 10¢, 11¢, 20¢, 3¢, 21¢, 30¢

**166–167** 21¢, 31¢, 30¢, 25¢, 35¢, 32¢, 50¢, 41¢, 52¢, 45¢, 17¢, 40¢

**168–169** Circle: 2 pennies, 2 quarters; dime, 2 quarters; nickel, 2 dimes, 2 quarters; dime, 3 quarters; 2 pennies, dime, quarter; all the coins; 3 pennies, dime, 2 quarters; penny, 2 dimes, 2 quarters; nickel, 2 quarters.

**170–171** 55¢/fifty-five cents, 90¢/ninety cents, 71¢/seventy-one cents, 44¢/forty-four cents, 1¢/one cent, 25¢/twenty-five cents, 20¢/twenty cents, 32¢/thirty-two cents, 15¢/fifteen cents, 63¢/sixty-three cents, 19¢/nineteen cents

**172–173** true, false, false, true, true, false, true, false, true, false, true, false

**174–175** >, <, >, =, >,<, =, =, >, >, =, >, =, >, <, =

**176–177** See below.

**178–179** night or day, day, night, day, night, night, day, day, day, day, day, night; 4

**180–181** 10, 10:00; 9, 9:00; 1, 1:00; 2, 2:00; 6, 6:00; 11, 11:00; 7, 7:00; 8, 8:00, 5, 5:00

**182–183** 8 o'clock; 9 o'clock; 10 o'clock, 12 o'clock; 1 o'clock; 2 o'clock; 3 o'clock; 4 o'clock; 5 o'clock; 6 o'clock; 7 o'clock, 8 o'clock; 9 o'clock

**184–185** See below.; time and answers will vary.

**186–187** two, 2:30; five, 5:30; four, 4:30; six, 6:30; twelve, 12:30; eight, 8:30; nine, 9:30; one, 1:30; three, 3:30; eleven, 11:30; ten, 10:30

**188–189** See below.

**190–191** middle, first, last; first, last, middle; last, first, middle; last, middle, first; middle, first, last; first, last, middle

**192–193** See below.

**194–195** 25¢, 32¢, 35¢, 35¢, Adam, Ella

**196** yes: 2 dimes, 1 nickel; yes: 2 quarters, 1 dime; yes: 3 dimes; yes: 2 nickels, 1 dime; yes: 1 quarter, 1 dime, 1 nickel; yes: 1 quarter, 2 dimes; yes: 2 quarters, 1 nickel; yes: 1 quarter, 2 nickels

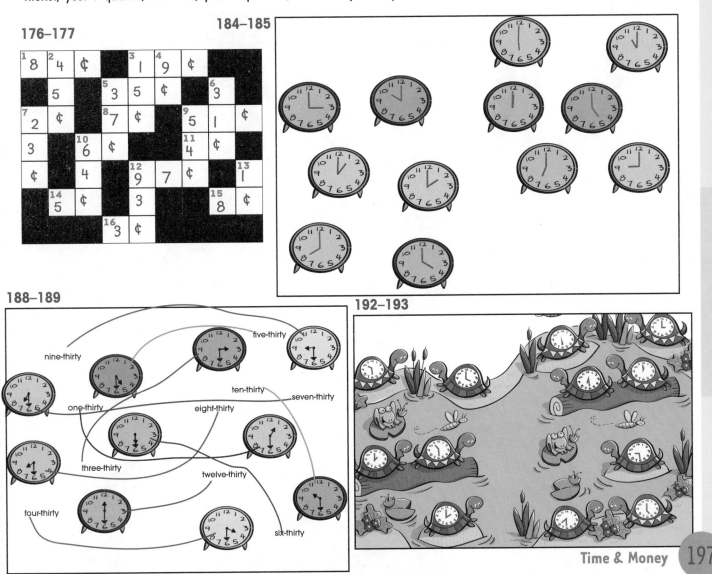

**176–177**

**184–185**

**188–189**

**192–193**

# Something in Common

(Circle) all the things that are the same color. Use that color
crayon or marker to make your circles.

Underline all the things you can eat.

Put an **X** near all the tools or things that
help you do something.

Put a **1** near all the things with numbers on them.

Draw a rectangle around all the things that live outside.

How many things are or were alive? _____

How many things are round? _____

How many things would you find in a kitchen? _____

# Mixed-Up Match Up

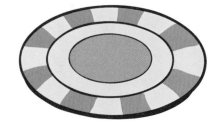

# Draw a line between each pair that belongs together.

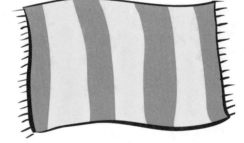

# Having a Ball

This pictograph shows all of the balls at the playground.
Look at the pictograph. Answer the questions.

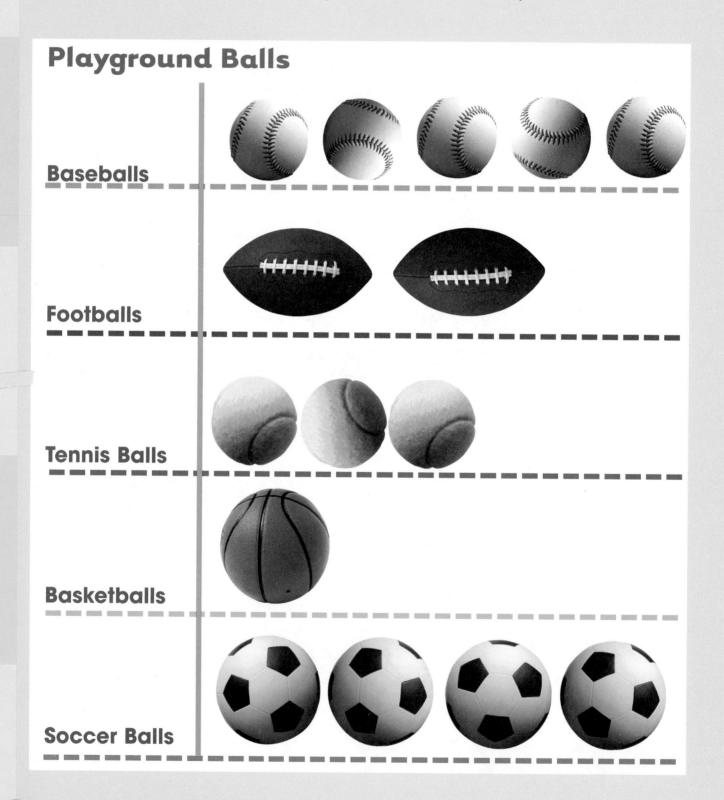

**Playground Balls**

Baseballs

Footballs

Tennis Balls

Basketballs

Soccer Balls

1. What is the title of this pictograph? _____

2. How many 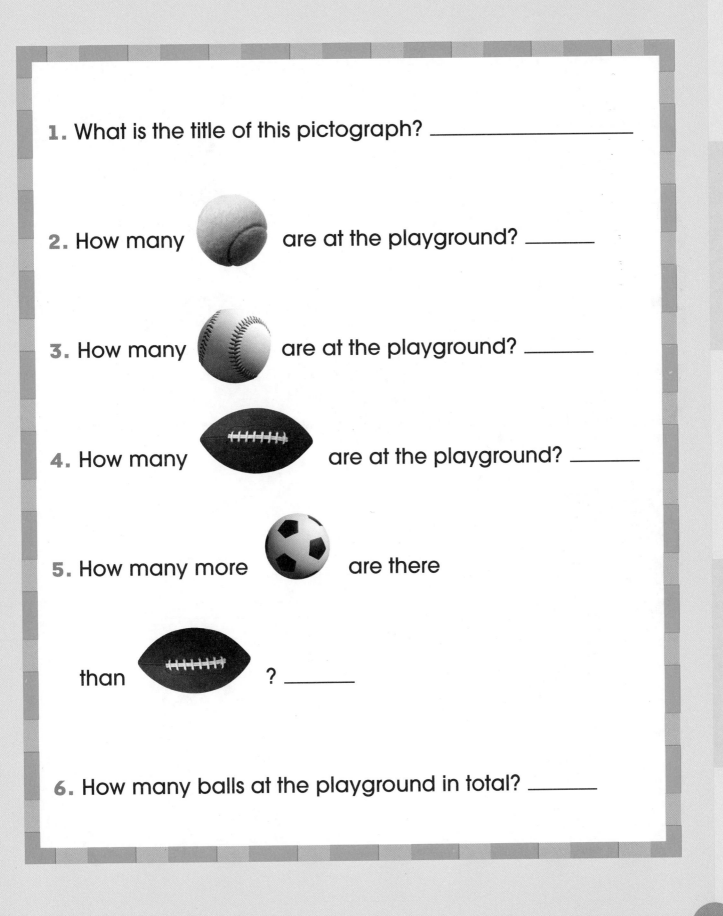 are at the playground? _____

3. How many are at the playground? _____

4. How many are at the playground? _____

5. How many more are there

than ? _____

6. How many balls at the playground in total? _____

# Pick a Pizza

Draw 3 different toppings on each pizza. List the toppings below each pizza. Can you make 5 kinds of pizza?

## Pizza Toppings

pepperoni

peppers

onions

olives

mushrooms

Pizza 1

_____

_____

_____

Pizza 2

_____

_____

_____

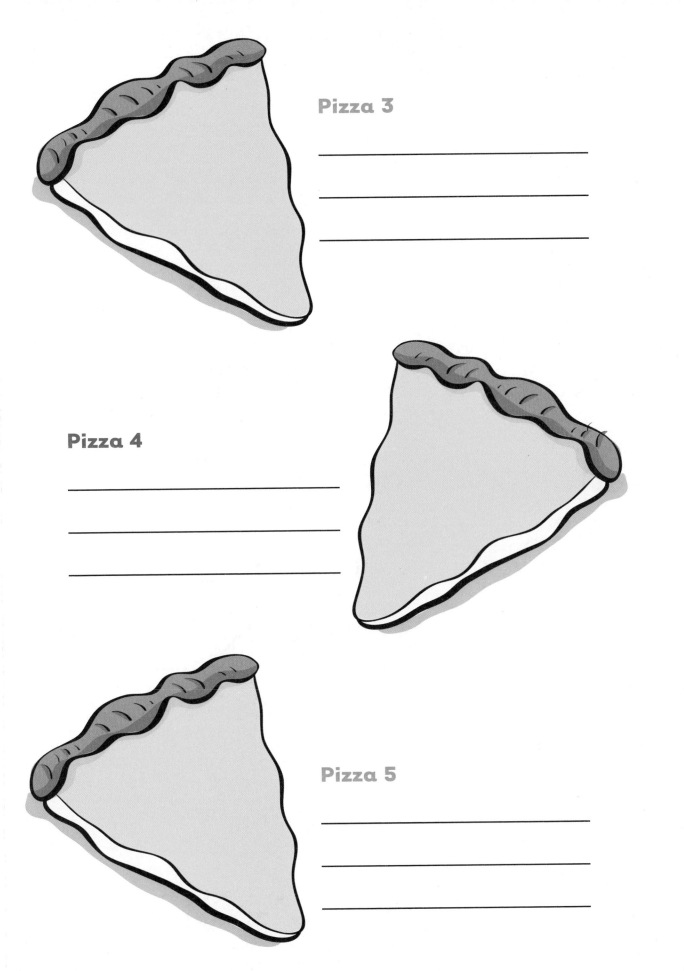

**Pizza 3**

_____

_____

_____

**Pizza 4**

_____

_____

_____

**Pizza 5**

_____

_____

_____

# Tally Rally

You can use tally marks to keep track of amounts.

Tally marks are grouped by 5s, like this: 卌.

What do these tally marks stand for? Write the number.

卌 _____          卌 卌 _____

卌 卌 卌 卌 _____          卌 卌 卌 _____

卌 卌 卌 卌 卌 _____

卌 卌 卌 卌 卌 卌 _____

卌 卌 卌 卌 卌 卌 卌 _____

卌 卌 卌 卌 卌 卌 卌 _____

卌 卌 卌 卌 卌 卌 卌 卌 卌 卌 _____

卌 卌 卌 卌 卌 卌 卌 卌 卌 _____

If you're tallying something that doesn't evenly group by five, you will have leftover lines.

These tally marks equal 7: 卌 ||

Write the tally marks for these numbers.

5

8

6

10

12

16

20

23

27

# Apples for Sale!

This pictograph shows the fruit Tom sold
at his market in one week. Look at the pictograph.
Answer the questions.

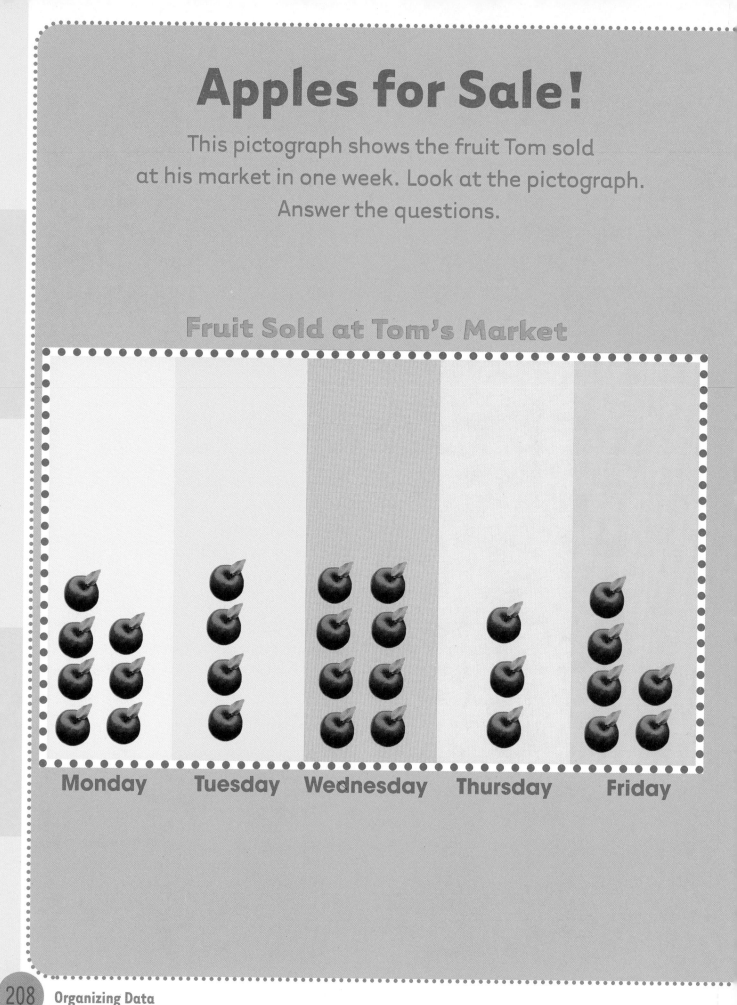

Fruit Sold at Tom's Market

Monday   Tuesday   Wednesday   Thursday   Friday

Organizing Data

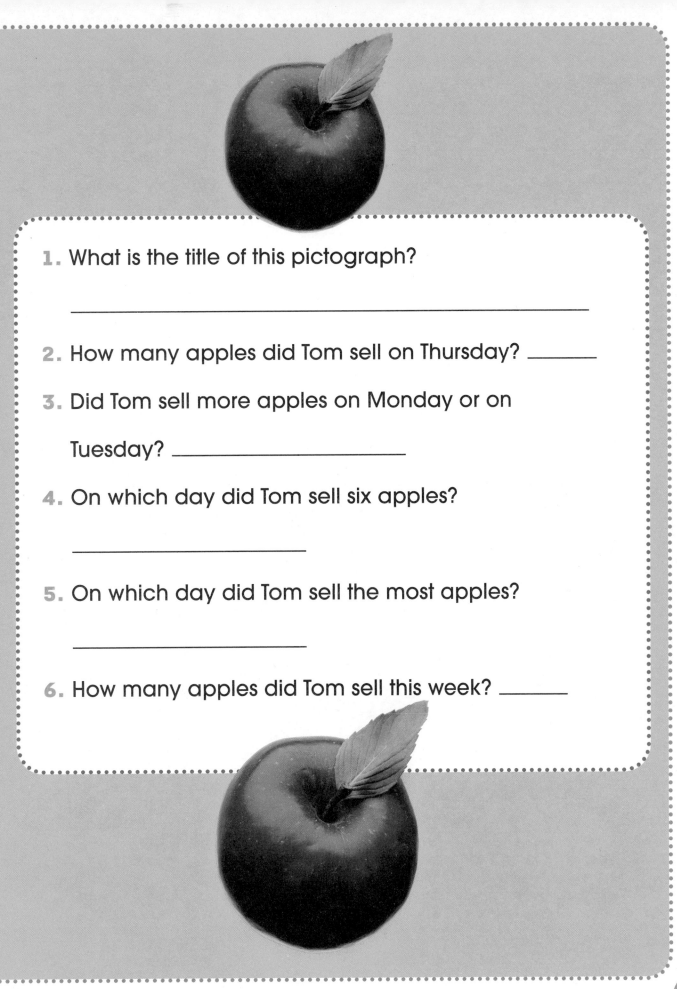

1. What is the title of this pictograph?

   _____

2. How many apples did Tom sell on Thursday? _____

3. Did Tom sell more apples on Monday or on

   Tuesday? _____

4. On which day did Tom sell six apples?

   _____

5. On which day did Tom sell the most apples?

   _____

6. How many apples did Tom sell this week? _____

# Math Hats

Put on your math thinking cap.
Write the numbers from the hats that . . .

have at least one 3 _____ _____ _____ _____

are less than 10 _____ _____ _____

are greater than 50 _____ _____ _____ _____

33

30

4

10

7

11

99

66

43

have both 10s and 1s _____ _____ _____ _____ _____

_____ _____ _____ _____

end in 0 _____ _____ _____ _____

have 2 of the same digit _____ _____ _____ _____ _____

100

80

3

# Repeat After Me

Draw the next parts of each pattern.

A B A B A ___ ___ ___ ___

3 4 5 3 4 5 3 4 5 ___ ___ ___

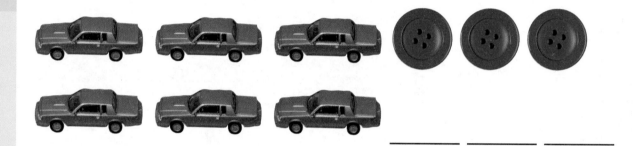
___ ___ ___

K K T T K K T T ___ ___ ___ ___ ___

___ ___ ___

8 2 2 8 2 2 8 2 2

___ ___ ___

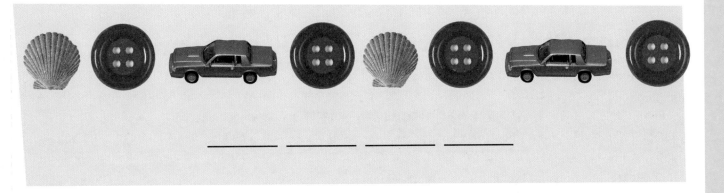

___ ___ ___ ___

CCMCCMCCM___ ___ ___

___ ___ ___

BBJBBWBBJBBW

___ ___ ___

# Morning Math

Mrs. Rossi's class made a bar graph.
It shows what the class ate for breakfast.
Look at the bar graph. Answer the questions.

## What Did We Eat for Breakfast Today?

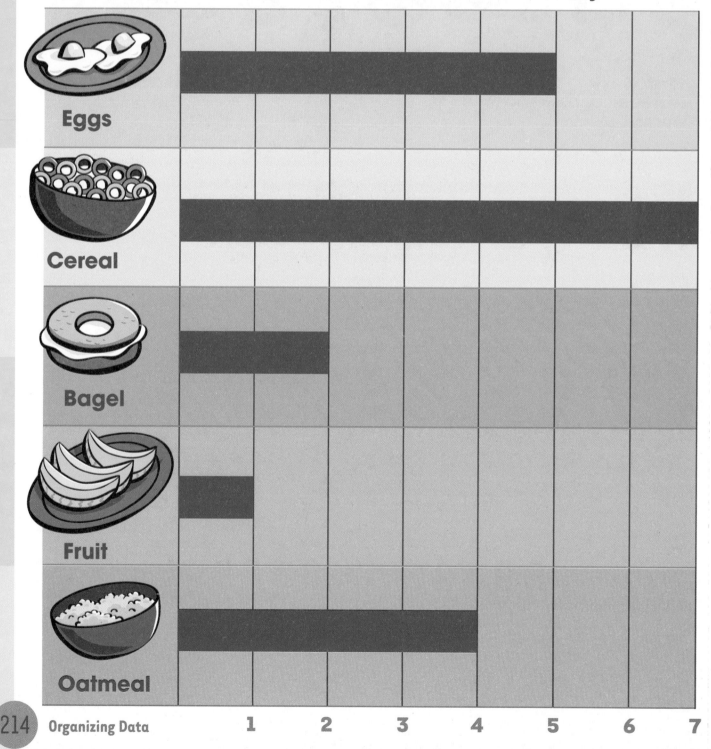

|  | 1 | 2 | 3 | 4 | 5 | 6 | 7 |
|---|---|---|---|---|---|---|---|
| Eggs | | | | | | | |
| Cereal | | | | | | | |
| Bagel | | | | | | | |
| Fruit | | | | | | | |
| Oatmeal | | | | | | | |

1. What is the title of this bar graph?

   _____

2. How many students ate oatmeal? _____

3. How many students ate fruit? _____

4. Which food did five students eat? _____

5. Which food did the most students eat?

   _____

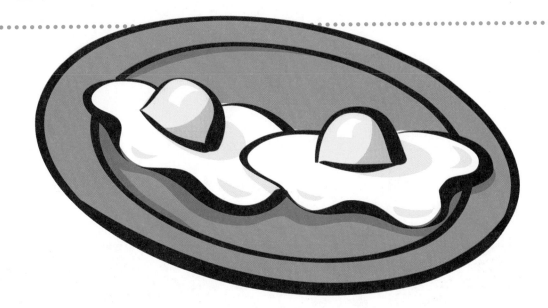

# Tallyho!

Count by fives to add up the tally marks.
Answer the questions.

## Horses at Star Ranch

**Barn 1**  |||| |

**Barn 2**  |||| | |||| | |||| | |||| | |||| | |||| |

**Barn 3**  |||| | |||| | |||| | |||| |

**Barn 4**  |||| | |||| | |||| | |||| | |||| |

**Barn 5**  |||| | |||| | |||| |

**Barn 6**  |||| | |||| |

1. What is the title of this graph?

   _____

2. How many horses are in Barn 5? _____

3. How many horses are in Barn 2? _____

4. Which barn has 20 horses in it? _____

5. How many horses are in Barn 1 and Barn 6? _____

6. How many horses are at Star Ranch? _____

# Picture This

Turtle and his friends started to make a pictograph. Read the facts on page 219. Use the facts to fill in the missing parts by drawing books.

Organizing Data

1. The title of the pictograph is

   "How Many Books Did We Read?"

2. Elephant read three books.

3. Rabbit read four books.

4. Turtle read five books.

5. Mouse and cat read five books each.

6. Rabbit read one more book than elephant did.

7. Bat took a nap and didn't read any books!

| Elephant | |
| --- | --- |
| Rabbit | |
| Turtle | |
| Mouse | |
| Cat | |
| Bat | |

# Movie Mania

The families on Oak Street made a bar graph.
It shows how many movies each family rented in one month.
Look at the bar graph. Answer the questions.

# Movie Rentals on Oak Street Last Month

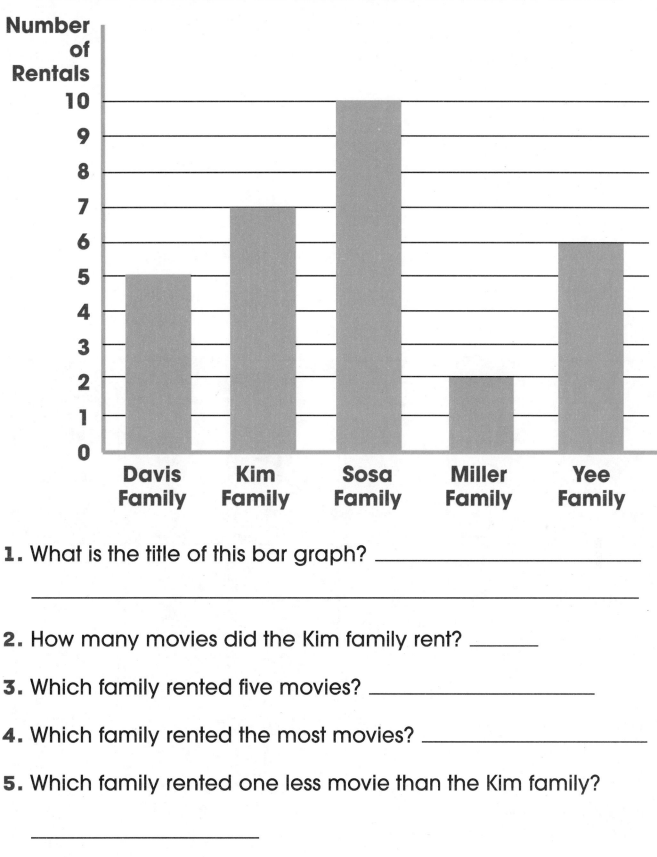

**Number of Rentals**

Davis Family — Kim Family — Sosa Family — Miller Family — Yee Family

1. What is the title of this bar graph? _____

_____

2. How many movies did the Kim family rent? _____

3. Which family rented five movies? _____

4. Which family rented the most movies? _____

5. Which family rented one less movie than the Kim family?

_____

6. How many movies were rented in all? _____

# Match!

You will need two players. Cut out the cards.

**Rules**

Put the cards facedown in a pile.

Deal two cards at a time.

The cards can match by shape, color, or design.

The first person to see a match yells, "Match!" and gets 1 point.

If there is no match, the cards go back in the pile.

The first person to get 10 points wins.

## Organizing Data Answer Key

**198–199** **Circle** button, watermelon, apple, die; **underline** cookie, banana, cupcake, watermelon, apple, cake; **put an X on** the balls, roller blades, hammer, bucket; **put a 1 near** the stamp; 5; 4; answers will vary.

**200–201** See below.

**202–203** 1. Playground Balls, 2. 3, 3. 5, 4. 2, 5. 2, 6. 15

**204–205** 10 possible combinations are: pepperoni/onions/mushrooms; onions/mushrooms/peppers; mushrooms/peppers/olives; pepperoni/mushrooms/olives; pepperoni/mushrooms/peppers; onions/mushrooms/olives; onions/peppers/olives; pepperoni/onions/olives; pepperoni/peppers/olives; pepperoni/onions/peppers.

**206–207** 5, 10, 20, 15, 25, 30, 40, 35, 50, 45; **see below.**

**208–209** 1. Fruit Sold at Tom's Market, 2. 3, 3. on Monday, 4. Friday, 5. Wednesday, 6. 28

**210–211** 33, 30, 43, 3; 4, 7, 3; 99, 66, 100, 80; 33, 30,10, 11, 99, 66, 43, 80, 100; 10, 30, 80, 100; 33, 99, 66, 11, 100

**212–213** B, A, B, A; 3, 4, 5; button, button, button; K, K, T, T; cookie, shell, button; 8, 2, 2; shell, button, toy car, button; C, C, M; button, shell, cookie, cookie; B, B, J

**214–215** 1. What Did We Eat For Breakfast Today? 2. 4, 3. 1, 4. eggs, 5. cereal

**216–217** 1. Horses at Star Ranch, 2. 15, 3. 30, 4. Barn 3, 5. 15, 6. 105

**218–219** See below.

**220–221** 1. Movie Rentals on Oak Street Last Month, 2. 7, 3. the Davis family, 4. the Sosa family, 5. the Yee family, 6. 30

**200–201**

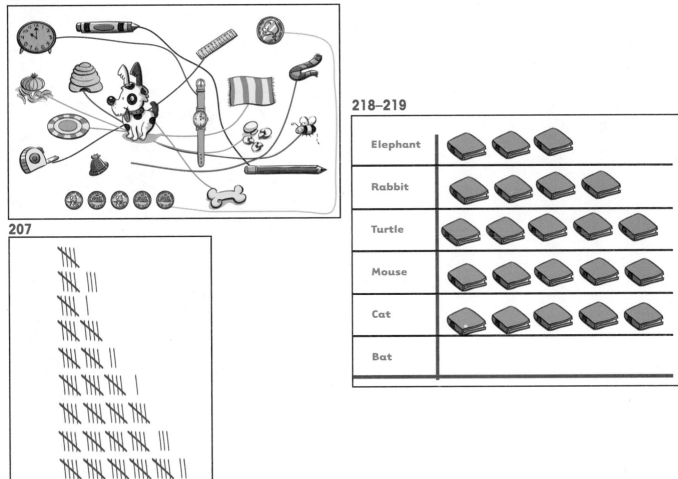

**207**

**218–219**

# Math Skills

These essential math skill are covered in the following activity pages.

## Number Sense

**comparing quantities** (more/less) 38–39, 40–41; (greater than/less than/equal to) 42–43, 44–45, 46–47, 48–49

**counting** 8–9, 18–19, 20–21, 24–25

**even/odd numbers** 52–53

**number order** 14–15, 26–27

**number recognition** 4–5, 6–7, 12–13, 16–17, 22–23

**number words** 10–11, 12–13, 16–17, 22–23, 50–51, 54–55

**place value: tens, ones** 34–35, 36–37, 48–49, 54–55

**skip-counting** (2s) 28–29; (5s) 30–31; (10s) 32–33

## Addition & Subtraction

**addition** 58–59, 60–61, 62–63, 64–65, 66–67, 68–69, 70–71, 72–73, 80–81, 82–83, 84–85, 86–87, 88–89, 92–93, 94–95, 96–97, 98–99, 104–105, 112–113, 114

**addition of 3 numbers** 100–101, 102–103, 104–105, 112–113

**2-digit addition** 106–107, 110–111, 112–113

**fact families** 80–81

**subtraction** 74–75, 76–77, 78–79, 80–81, 82–83, 84–85, 86–87, 88–89, 90–91, 92–93, 94–95, 96–97, 98–99, 112–113, 114

**2-digit subtraction** 108–109, 110–111, 112–113

## Measurement

**comparing length** 122–123

**comparing size** 116–117, 118–119, 126–127, 138

**comparing weight** 116–117

**comparing volume** 124–125

**days, month, calendar** 128–129, 130–131

**measuring tools** 120–121

**standard measurements** (inches) 134–135, 136–137

**temperature** 132–133

## Geometry

**directional words** 140–141

**shape patterns** 152–153, 160

**shape recognition** 142–143, 144–145, 146–147, 148–149, 150–151, 152–153, 154–155, 156–157, 160

**solid shapes** 158, 159

## Time & Money

**adding money** 164–165, 166–167

**identifying coins, amounts, money words** 162–163, 168–169, 170–171, 172–173, 176–177, 194–195, 196

**comparing money** (greater than/less than/equal to) 174–175

**comparing day/night** 178–179

**telling time** (hours) 180–181, 182–183, 184–185, 190–191, 192–193; (half-hour) 186–187, 188–189, 190–191, 192–193

## Organizing Data

**bar graphs** 214–215, 220–221

**comparing information** 210–211

**patterns** 212–213

**pictographs** 202–203, 208–209, 218–219

**sorting** 198–199, 200–201, 204–205

**tallying** 206–207, 216–217